The New Dean's Survival Guide:

Advice from An Academic Leader

By Thomas R. McDaniel

MAGNA

Magna Publications
Madison, Wisconsin

Magna Publications
2718 Dryden Drive
Madison, WI 53704
Magnapubs.com

The articles in this book have been previously published in the *Academic Leader* newsletter or the *Faculty Focus* blog.

ISBN: 978-0-912150-70-3

Contents

Introduction

With the fine editorial assistance of the professional staff at Magna Publications, which publishes *Academic Leader*, *Faculty Focus*, and many other excellent support sources for college administrators, I have assembled selected essays from ones I have published in *Academic Leader* (as well as one from *Faculty Focus*) to serve as this survival guide for new academic deans. Most of these essays are brief examinations of selected topics I found important, or at least interesting, for my work in various leadership roles at my liberal arts college, which now hosts nine graduate degree programs—many of which I initiated, implemented, and nurtured—as well as four undergraduate degree programs.

Before retiring in 2015 (but still teaching a graduate course in school law for administrators), I held such positions as associate director of a master's degree program at a major university, Johns Hopkins University, and then at a liberal arts institution, Converse College in South Carolina. My positions at Converse included department chair, division head, dean of the College of Arts and Sciences, acting dean of the School of Education and Graduate Studies, vice president for academic affairs, provost, interim president, and (finally) senior vice president. During all those administrative appointments over a span of 50 years, I always taught at least three or four courses per year and kept an active speaking and writing agenda, with more than 100 speeches and conference presentations and 300 publications. Note: Here I am describing, not bragging, to let you know it is possible to walk and chew gum at the same time—and to lead and teach at the same time as well. I sure made my share of mistakes along the way, but that is inevitable for academic leaders everywhere. I tried to learn from these mistakes.

I present the selected essays that follow to help new deans avoid some of my errors and to develop a positive and productive approach to the fine art of *deaning* (not a real word, but it should be!). I have organized these essays to more or less mirror the trajectory of a dean's career in office: they begin with early considerations of what is required personally and professionally when one applies for the job, and they conclude by addressing how to wind down one's career. There's lots to think about along that long and interesting career path!

In Chapter 1 I have chosen essays that may help you think about whether this leadership position is right for you. In most cases you will have to decide to pursue the possibility by searching job postings in publications such as the *Journal of Higher Education* and *The Chronicle of Higher Education* or responding to online postings for such positions; in other cases, as was true for me, a provost or president at your own institution might encourage you to apply for open positions there—a possibility made especially attractive by your being able to stay right where you are, with no disruptive moving from your happy home should you succeed in that search process. That you have been encouraged by a prospective boss and established relationships with faculty can be an advantage as well—but changing those relationships offers its own special challenges.

If you are now beginning your new job as a dean, you may have already considered some of the matters introduced in articles like "The 'Quiet' Dean," based on a book by Susan Cain titled *Quiet: The Power of Introverts in a World That Can't Stop Talking.* In this essay I raise the personality concern some quiet, even introverted, faculty may have as to whether less outgoing yet more reflective individuals can serve effectively when popular stereotypes of the bold, assertive, take-charge dean are the norm. I tend toward that reflective style myself, so take comfort in analysis that supports the value of the quiet approach to leadership.

A related justification is found in the ancient philosophy of Taoism. In his famous *Tao Te Ching,* Lao Tzu gives guidance to the leaders of Chinese society of 2,500 years ago that has merit for leadership behavior today. He advocates leadership that is gentle and proclaims that "the quality of silence conveys more than long speeches"—music to my ears and maybe yours. Consider this ancient wisdom as you read "The Tao of Deaning." It took me some time to realize that there are costs to leadership, and I spell out some of those in another article in this opening chapter that might give you pause. But not to worry. Leadership also pays, and not just in the higher salary you should receive as you move from a faculty position to the deanship. Weigh the costs and rewards of the dean's role as you begin your search and service. "Servant leadership" is a worthy concept to build your legacy on.

You do not want to make the mistake of assuming your being an amazingly good professor will assure your success as a dean. You do continue teaching—not just students but the faculty as well—when you are dean. But leadership requires far more than teaching ability. "When Good Professors Turn into Bad Deans" examines that conundrum. This essay was written in response to a professor-reader of my Dean's Dialogue column in *Academic Leader* who mildly complained that I had lots of advice for how deans might deal with contrary and unhappy faculty but nothing at all about legitimate complaints a professor might have about another professor who becomes dean and then goes over "to the dark side" to wreak havoc on former colleagues in the faculty—a point I had to concede and tried to address in this article.

The other essays in Chapter 1 are self-evident: your role as a leader, delegator, and faculty morale booster require constant attention, and I hope some ideas in these essays help you formulate your own thoughts about mastering such duties of office. "Leading the Faculty: A Dean's Definition" summarizes much of my own thinking on what a new dean should know about the administrative role they will play in the college or university. I wish some former dean had told me all this at the start of my career!

In Chapter 2 I include some of my most practical advice for new deans, starting with two essays on your dean's "toolbox." A hammer, saw, drill, and C-clamp might sound like instruments of torture, but they need not be! (I did not include a blowtorch, as you will discover.) The metaphors herein focus on day-to-day problems every leader will encounter in the workplace, and I hope to have suggested some positive and constructive uses for each of these metaphorical tools. I presented the first toolbox essay at one of the annual Leadership in Higher Education conferences Magna offers, and I heartily commend these excellent gatherings of colleagues to you; at the conclusion of my session, I asked the attendees to suggest other tools of value, which led me to add more instruments to the leader's tools of the trade ("More Tools for the New Dean's Toolbox"). Like most of my *Academic Leader* essays, this one required no actual research (not my strong suit, I confess).

Some of the advice articles in this chapter were inspired by things I read, like my piece on "Devilish Deaning," featuring none other than that devil incarnate Machiavelli—author of the classic advice in *The Prince* to maximize your leadership power by learning from the fox and the lion. I do not recommend Machiavelli as your role model, but do not reject everything he advises!

"The Power of Listening" will point you to another set of practical skills. Many communication experts offer advice on improving listening skills, and I think this might be one of the most valuable abilities any dean could aspire to master and practice. On the other side of the communication process, you will find in "Distorted Deaning" some useful suggestions on what you say in conversations with faculty and other administrators. Do you overgeneralize, take complaints personally, or engage in scaremongering, mind reading, black-and-white thinking, or name-calling? Maybe you overuse pressurizing terms like *must* and *should* or extremist words like *always*, *never*, and *nobody*. These are speaking and thinking problems that plague many administrators as they attempt to be authoritative. But you can eliminate such problems with focused practice in everyday communication and mindfulness as you monitor your own conversations.

I hope the advice in a companion essay on "Academic Leader as Communicator in Chief" will also prove helpful as you grow in your deanly communication skills. Those who speak with clarity, conviction, proper grammar, and few distracting words (like *so*, *well*, *you know*, and *I mean*) will be more successful than other speakers when it comes to getting their positions understood and accepted.

Chapters 3 and 4 present a number of specific issues I have had to deal with in the college administrative sphere; some of these will no doubt remain for years—like freedom of expression for students and faculty (even as legal requirements evolve), ongoing accreditation requirements for rigorous self-studies, and increasing demands by accreditors for objective data showing you have complied with the accrediting agencies' stated standards. I address such developments in the essay titled "Asssessmania and Bureaupathology in Higher Education." Take no offense at my metaphorical implications in "Surviving your Regional Accreditation." That essay is indeed a tongue-in-cheek venture.

Other issues might disappear or evolve, but I selected ones I thought were likely to be perennial concerns for those of us charged with the academic health of our institution. Other essays in these chapters should get you thinking about such issues as student evaluations of professors, president-faculty relations (which can sorely test a dean's patience), and the ways bureaucratic demands get in the way of teaching and learning—with all such issues too often ending up in your office. Do try to "discover your inner snail," as another essay recommends, and not overreact to such pressures.

Chapter 5, the final chapter in this survival guide, considers how your dean's career might end. Using the reflections of professor Randy Pausch in his famous talk titled "Achieving Your Childhood Dreams" (a.k.a. "The Last Lecture") at Carnegie Mellon University, I considered how I might go about writing "My Last Commencement Speech," an essay here that might prove useful ideas for you when it comes time to close the curtain on your dean's duties. But perhaps you will find the administrative life so rewarding that you look at climbing the administrative ladder even higher to become the institution's provost. In case you are not sure what a provost is, I try to answer that question in "So, What's a Provost?" In my case, that office—like my later interim president job—was thrust upon me (recalling Malvolio's claim in *Twelfth Night* that "some are born great, some achieve greatness, and some have greatness thrust upon them") by some unusual employment circumstances involving changes mandated by the board of trustees. Rest assured that I make no claim to greatness! Appointments to higher office that result from unanticipated circumstances happen more frequently than you might suspect.

But some of you may decide to go in another direction: back to the classroom, on to another deanship at bigger and better institution (because you have enjoyed what I called "Delightful Deaning"), off to become an accreditation agency evaluator of other higher education institutions, or into publishing or other businesses as an administrator or consultant. Your talent and visibility can open doors you never knocked on before. Even if you have considered my thoughts in "A Dean's Demise" and find yourself ready for the "Ongoing Life of One Retired Dean," perhaps one day you will write your own final thoughts—as I did in "Reflections of a Retired Dean." The decision to retire is one I hope you can make with confidence and the knowledge that you served your institution(s) well when you undertook the challenging and enjoyable (most days) dean's position years ago. That worked for me, and I hope it works for you too!

1

The "Quiet" Dean

Memo to academic leaders: I am sitting quietly in my dean's office, a serene place I first occupied in 1986, reflecting on a book by Susan Cain, one that I think you all should read, titled *Quiet: The Power of Introverts in a World That Can't Stop Talking* (2012). I would much rather communicate to you from my peaceful digs by way of a memo than to set forth my ideas in a sparkling speech at a conference. Perhaps like you—or perhaps not—I am an introvert and quick to admit it. Whether you are an introvert or an extrovert (and so many academic leaders now embody the extrovert ideal of our contemporary culture), you will find Cain's book informative, thoughtful, and (even) practical.

Let me at the outset ask you to reflect (introverts, after all, are reflective thinkers) on a few questions:

Do you know whether you are an introvert or an extrovert? If you have taken the Myers-Briggs Type Indicator Inventory or some similar self-assessment on personality, you may have already made that determination. As you know, extroverts tend to be energized by crowds and social interaction, quickly say whatever comes to mind, often think out loud, would rather talk than listen, and gravitate toward group work and committees where they can shine. They are comfortable with conflict but not solitude. As Cain observes, "We are told that to be great is to be bold, to be happy is to be sociable" (p. 3). Introverts are just the opposite—they prefer the quiet, contemplative life; listen well; and prefer to work individually. The contrast, to oversimplify, is between action-oriented, quick decision makers and solitude-oriented, cautious decision makers. Both can be effective leaders.

Are introversion and extroversion fixed personality traits or learned patterns of behavior? Early researchers, from Carl Jung (see his 1921 classic Psychological Types) onward, have argued that indeed introversion and extroversion are fixed traits, while more recent scholarship by a group of psychologists known as the Situationists suggests that there is no core self but "only the various selves of Situations X, Y, and Z" (Cain, 2012, p. 206). Nature-nurture debates still abound. Cain says that the most recent research concludes that there really is such a thing as a fixed personality, but some psychologists hold to the notion that these personality traits tend to occur in patterns, with some people being aggressive with subordinates but not so much with authority figures and others having opposite tendencies. And of course, there are continuums from extreme to moderate to mild on both concepts in the extroversion-introversion scale. I see myself as a moderate introvert.

Why has our contemporary society elevated the extrovert ideal? Now leaders are supposed to be high-energy risk-takers and out-front sales representatives for their ideas as well as for the institutional initiatives they are expected to advocate. Cain traces that evolution in our culture from the early efforts of spokesmen and authors such as Dale Carnegie (*How to Win Friends and Influence People*) to current management seminars by Tony Robbins and graduate degree programs such as the Harvard MBA. That we live in a world where personality and celebrity are constantly advanced by media pundits and social media outlets contributes to the ascendancy of the leader as extrovert. But Wharton management professor Adam Grant has conducted extensive research that shows the correlation between extroversion and leadership to be, at best, modest. In fact, Cain says, Grant's study concluded that introverted leaders "were more effective with proactive employees" and were especially effective in "advancing the great ideas of those they lead" (Cain, 2012, p. 56). They are especially good at supporting, nurturing, and advancing the great ideas of those they lead.

Why do institutions—and this would certainly include colleges and universities—need introverts in positions of significant leadership? This is where you and I enter the conversation. Cain argues that institutions that neglect the leadership skills of introverts are missing the boat.

Introverts in higher education leadership

Susan Cain, a professed introvert, left the hurly-burly of her work as a Wall Street lawyer to become an academic—not a college professor but one who would devote her time and effort to research and writing about introversion and extroversion. The academy has always been an attractive career option for introverts. That is natural because academic research and college teaching appeal to those who enjoy quiet study, the development of intellect, and what have traditionally been seen as the peaceful groves of academe. Cain points out that education in our time has increasingly focused on the extrovert ideal—group work, cooperative learning, leadership training, and the like. Most teachers, she notes, see the extrovert as the ideal student. Many professors continue to love the solitary life not only while living "in their heads" but also while sharing their insights in one-on-one interactions with students in small seminar classes and by writing for their disciplines.

Such individuals may even develop their skills as "pseudo extroverts," as Cain calls them, who can gear themselves up for large-class instruction and performance teaching—although such efforts often drain their energy. (By contrast, such interactions enhance the energy of extroverts.) Although introverts typically avoid self-promotion, they are sometimes recognized for their academic talents and promoted to positions as department chairs, deans, provosts, and presidents. They are, however, the exceptions.

Should you be one of those individuals, you might want to reflect on some of these ideas and strategies for being a successful academic leader:

Remember that the academic life is particularly dependent on thinkers. While academic leaders do have to be skilled at salesmanship, making quick decisions, handling group dynamics, and (even) self-promotion and the promotion of their most worthy ideas, the heart of the academy lies in developing the minds and the characters of their students. That is to say, the academic curriculum is inherently and substantively compatible with the talents of introverts.

Develop the pseudo-extrovert skills that will help you be successful as a leader. Cain says that "many people, especially those in leadership roles, engage in a certain level of pretend-extroversion" (p. 210). This is not the same as "faking it" but rather demonstrates that you can act decisively, speak confidently, and work harmoniously with those you lead. Introverts can develop "people skills" to help them become more effective leaders. Promoting harmony, listening well, and advancing the worthy ideas of others are useful introvert skills, but we cannot be hermits who isolate themselves from social interaction and tough decisions.

Learn how to talk with extroverts. Cain believes that "the two types are often drawn to each other—in friendship, business, and especially romance" (p. 224); as the old saying has it, opposites attract. We need each other and can complement one another—drawing on each other's strengths to form a more balanced whole. While introverts need not try to transform their own personalities to conform to the extrovert ideal of leadership, they can both develop their own communication strengths and develop helpful relationships with their extrovert counterparts.

Rely on your introvert strengths in rethinking the nature of leadership. For example, Cain points out that much of the essence of modern leadership depends on listening ability, at which introverts often excel. When it comes to negotiating, something all academic leaders have to do, "it often pays to be quiet and gracious, to listen more than to talk, and to have an instinct for harmony rather than conflict" (p. 216). Women as academic leaders often excel in this approach, a gentler style of leadership also advocated in classic texts by John Heider in *The Tao of Leadership* and by Linda Lambert and Mary Gardner in *Women's Ways of Leading*. Other books, such as *Quiet*, are advancing the intro-vert-as-leader mission: *Quiet Influence: The Introvert's Guide to Making a Difference* (2013), *Introverts at Ease: An Insider's Guide to a Great Life on Your Terms* (2011), and *The Quiet Guide for Getting Ahead* (2009)— to mention a few intriguing titles. Perhaps we are on the cusp of a new leadership paradigm! Good leaders know how to take strong positions without creating resentment and anger as they pour oil on troubled wa-ters, a common theme in all these works.

Promote balance, both in yourself and in your institution. At the individual level, introverts can find "restorative niches" when "you want to return to your true self." (p. 219). This can be a physical place as a retreat for solitude or even a psychological niche during a meeting. Extroverts who need a restorative niche after intense, isolated focus on a report can likewise schedule a social event to return to their true selves. Every academic institution needs both kinds of leaders—extroverts to excite the passions of passive faculty and introverts "who are uniquely good at leading initiative takers" (p. 57).

Although contemporary society tends to exalt the extrovert ideal for leaders (an aspect of a cultural shift in our dynamic, fast-paced world), academic leaders would do well to avoid the downsides of extroversion— unwarranted risk-taking, superficial salesmanship, and groupthink—while remembering that creativity and problem solving thrive in what Cain calls "the inner landscapes" of introverts, which "are rich and full of drama" (p. 266). Our extrovert colleagues and leaders can benefit from our differ-ent perspectives.

In our high-tech, change-oriented culture, privacy is almost nonex-istent, and quiet contemplation is a diminishing possibility for academic leaders. Or so it seems to us introverts. But don't fret. As Cain concludes,

"Introverts are offered keys to private gardens full of riches" (p. 266). Use those keys to open the door of academic leadership. Your institution needs your gifts.

Reference

Cain, S. (2012). *Quiet: The power of introverts in a world that can't stop talking.* New York, NY: Crown Publishing.

The Tao of Deaning

If Pooh's philosophy of life reflects the Tao, why shouldn't the dean's? That is to say, wise deans (like wise bears) may exemplify an approach to leadership and life that is reflective—in the fullest sense of the term—of values consistent with this ancient Chinese philosophy. After all, Lao Tzu formulated his ideas, as reported in the 5,000-word *Tao Te Ching*, to give guidance to the leaders of that society 2,500 years ago. The best deans I know today capture elements of Taoist thought in what they say and do. How about you?

The ancient author and his book

Lao, whose name is a title meaning something like "the grand old master," lived a simple life in fifth century BC China; he was a shadowy figure about whom little is known for certain. He was probably a recluse, a meditative thinker, and an archivist who was saddened by his people's disinclination to cultivate their natural goodness. Tradition says he wrote down his thoughts in three days on his way out of town on a water buffalo. His reflections on leadership and life can be read in 30 minutes but take a lifetime to understand fully and to apply wisely.

The *Tao Te Ching* has been translated more often than any book except the Bible. Its title means "The Way and Its Power" or "How Things Work," and its basic premise (if I may simplify) is as follows: to lead wisely, one must seek personal balance and harmony with the creative force that is in all of nature; be attuned to the inner rhythms of human nature, which connect to the flow and pattern of energy in the universe; and listen for the inner truth and wisdom that transcends the conflict and turmoil of noisy human organizations. Such is the way to peace—and power.

What has the Tao to do with deaning?

My life as a dean (you might say) is filled with conflict and confusion—with noise from above and below, with demands to shake things up, to make change, to establish new programs and eliminate old ones, and to be bold, strong, and decisive so that my leadership power and skills will be evident, energizing, and effective. It is my role, you might contend, to make waves and exercise my wise will on a recalcitrant faculty.

Not so, says Taoism: Quite the contrary

While the Tao Te Ching is a nonprescriptive set of meditations on how a person can find peace by living in cooperation with nature's law of harmony, there are some specific lessons for leadership that deans should heed. These lessons ask you to stress being over doing, listening over talking, and discerning the will of others over imposing your will on the group. Such lessons run counter to conventional wisdom about "decisive deaning." Here are three lessons—drawn from John Heider's translation, *The Tao of Leadership*—that I invite you to consider:

A journey of a thousand miles begins with a single step. One of Lao's most famous principles of leadership, this idea reminds deans to start small—and to start. How much do we undermine our effectiveness by procrastination, by waiting for more information, by working on grand designs when what we ought to do is just begin? "Continuous improvement," in small steps, is a key concept of total quality management, a leadership principle with merit. What "single steps" should you be taking?

The wise leader knows that yielding overcomes resistance and gentleness melts rigid defenses. Like water, says Lao, the "leader does not fight the force of the group's energy but flows and yields and absorbs and lets go. The ability to be soft makes the leader a leader. . . . What is soft is strong." How difficult this is for the modern dean who thinks being strong requires being resolute and implacable! This is the yin side of the yin-yang symbol for balanced leadership. Can you go with the flow?

The quality of one's silence conveys more than long speeches. We who lead like to hear ourselves talk. Why be silent when we can fill the air with profound and persuasive proclamations? Besides, if we are talking, others will have to listen. And if they listen well, they may see things the way we want them to. But, says Lao, that is about winning, not leading. Leading requires creative listening. Do you use the power of listening to be a better administrator?

For deans who are willing to listen and to learn—for "the wise leader is quiet and reflective"— the Tao of Deaning offers new possibilities for leadership practices rarely seen on college campuses in our time.

The Cost of Leadership

As a recently retired academic leader—a former department chair, division head, dean, vice president, provost, and interim president—I have had time to reflect on the joys and woes of leadership at a small liberal arts college. What successes did I have? What failures? What could I have done differently that would have made my college a better institution? "Too soon old and too late smart," an old saying goes. But there is some value in ex post facto assessments, yes?

If one looks at the academic leader balance sheet, what kinds of accounting might one find? Below I identify four principles that might help other deans and college administrators evaluate the pluses and minuses of the leadership dynamic.

Principle 1: It isn't easy being dean

There are those in the academy—often professors and staff members working in the trenches—who think their leaders have it easy: a big office, good pay and benefits, and underlings to whom the hard work can be delegated. But with apologies to Kermit the Frog (who was lamenting color discrimination), it isn't easy being dean, a position that has many pains as well as pleasures: hiring and keeping that cadre of "trench workers," managing complex and limited budgets, and dealing with unhappy students—and even worse, their parents—can make a long work week even longer and more painful. No, it is not easy being dean!

Principle 2: No good dean goes unpunished

This principle of leadership follows from the first. If the dean (or other academic leader) makes a decision that is controversial or unpopular or both, that leader should be ready to "suffer the slings and arrows of outrageous fortune" (with apologies this time to the Bard). How is such punishment to be delivered? Oh, let me count the ways! There is gossip, ostracizing, memos to superiors (or even to the local newspaper), angry recriminations, hanging in effigy, no-confidence votes—the list of punishments is long indeed. Perhaps we should ignore what we can on the grounds that what other people think of you is none of your business, or perhaps we should counter what we can and dismiss the rest on the basis of Yogi Berra's wise comment: "Half the lies people tell about me aren't true." And face it: we deserve some of the punishments that come our way, and some pain is therapeutic.

Principle 3: The lead administrator has the best view

This principle comes from the world of dog sleds and canine leadership, but it has its application in higher education as well. Those at the back of the pack will usually have their view limited by those at the front. Such perspectives always influence points of view. A related principle says, "Where you stand depends on where you sit." In any event, the leader has a more or less unrestricted view of the terrain ahead. How will government policies affect anticipated resources? How will MOOCs and other technological innovations affect enrollments in brick-and-mortar colleges? What important new trends can we see emerging from the murky mist of college reform efforts elsewhere? Decisions by academic leaders have to reflect the long view and the big picture—and consider the likely costs. Some of those costs are the natural aftermath of change, but we must not, as futurist Joel Barker warned, mistake the edge of our rut for the horizon.

Principle 4: Academic leadership costs, but it also pays

Making decisions about the direction of one's institution will always have consequences, whether positive or negative or both. Instituting a new academic program, major, certificate credential, or travel-study opportunity for students—any such decision will create a host of winners and losers. A new academic major, for example, will help recruit new students to the college, but it may also create collateral damage: fewer students choosing existing academic majors. Eliminating an existing academic resource—a writing center, for example—can help balance the budget but at a cost of jobs and student academic performance. So much of academic leadership is making win-lose decisions; you can only aim for as many win-win decisions as possible.

No doubt: when I was leading a department, a division, a school, or the college, I made both good and poor decisions. My vision now, in hindsight, is 20/30 if not 20/20. But decisions have to be made in the confusing context of the present. In some cases I was too slow to act and in others too quick. In still other cases I needed to secure more buy-in and better information before moving ahead. But that is the fate of any academic leader.

Those of us privileged to occupy a position of leadership in our institutions can only work to calculate the costs and benefits of any decision we are required to make. Then we should do all we can to make it work for the people and colleges we serve. That is our task—a more difficult one than most of our critics know.

When Good Professors Turn into Bad Deans

"Thanks for your 'Dean's Dialogue' columns, Tom—you offer some good advice to deans and other administrators. But it seems like your deans are always noble and virtuous while the faculty they lead are villains and miscreants. What happens when good professors turn into bad deans?"

This was the gist of an email comment I received from a chemistry professor. He had run across some of my columns that I wrote for *Academic Leader* a few years ago (notably "The Dean's Dirty Dozen," a list of stereotypes of faculty who make a dean's life difficult—reprinted later in this volume) and sent a plaintive message of concern after dealing with a fine professor in his department who had risen (or descended, if you prefer) to the dean's office. "She was highly regarded as a teacher and scholar," my correspondent continued, "but as dean she has proved herself to be arrogant, distant, self-serving, and a poor communicator to those of us she left behind in the academic trenches. She spent lots of money redecorating her new office and seems to have her eye on an even more exalted post at our university—or elsewhere. She has been a disaster!"

I wasn't sure how to reply except to thank him for writing and to say I felt his pain. It is true, of course, that we who have been in the deaning business have some marvelous faculty colleagues to sustain our collective efforts to make our institutions work effectively. I also confess to an assumption that those who rise to the deanship are usually well motivated and well qualified to serve in their leadership positions. But what do you do in those rare cases when the dean is a disaster? Why do some great professors become poor academic deans? Let me try to answer both of these questions, starting with the second one.

Why good professors may morph into bad deans

There are, no doubt, many explanations for this unfortunate transformation. Here are just a few to consider:

The professor paradigm. What makes a great professor? There is no single formula, of course, but most of the best professors are intelligent, creative, and personable. They bring those qualities to bear in their work with students and with their scholarly endeavors. These qualities also serve to make them good administrators. But good professors' egos may also drive them to shine in the public domain and to gain recognition from their adoring students. They may also be highly idiosyncratic, better as lone ranger scholars than as team players. When dean search committees fail to see how certain candidates may be characterized more by a desire for power and recognition than by their better angels, good professors may turn into ineffective deans.

The perception problem. In some cases both deans and faculty misperceive the role and performance of the academic dean. Female deans continue to have a heavier burden in winning acceptance in leadership positions. The male dean may be seen as assertive, while the female dean is seen as bossy. That gender discrimination problem is changing but still lingers. Deans may also fall victim to a misperception that they should see their faculty as employees to be directed and supervised as the dean sees fit. That may be true to a point—but only to a point. Good deans know how to use the principles of effective communication to counteract such misperceptions by faculty, but some deans used to commanding students' loyalty and compliance fail to appreciate the collegial nature of working in the academy.

The president-provost priorities conundrum. Often enough (sometimes too often) the dean is caught between serving the needs of the faculty and meeting the priorities of their own leaders: the provost and the president. Faculty may or may not be aware of those priorities or may not see them as important for their own work. In many cases the dean feels the squeeze and does not have the ability to navigate the chasm. Perhaps this conflict of priorities is most often manifest in budget decisions. Faculty frequently see the dean's role as one of providing resources for all manner of faculty priorities— released time, research, travel—while the provost and president are desperately trying to keep the budget balanced. The dean who is unable to satisfy two masters both cheerfully and with good grace will soon lose the confidence of one master or the other.

The Peter principle. Lest we forget, studies of the organizational hierarchy have observed that as people move up the ladder in any bureaucracy, including colleges and universities, the demands of office expose their weaknesses for more and more observers to criticize. In some sense deans do rise to their level of incompetency. As John McEnroe put it so inelegantly, "The higher the monkey climbs the flagpole, the more people there are who see his rear end." Very fine professors may simply lack the administrative skills—from budget management to personnel supervision to diplomacy to decision-making—that the deanship requires.

What do you do when good professors become bad deans?

This is not an easy question to answer. Faculty may have to grin and bear it, at least for a while, in hopes that the dean will see the light or move on to some other institution where the fit may be better for dean and faculty alike. Here are a few possible approaches to consider if those changes do not magically appear:

The dean intervention process. It may be that faculty leaders, perhaps from the faculty senate, should seek a hearing with the dean to clear the air and offer sound managerial advice from the faculty perspective. If handled discretely in a nonconfrontational fashion, such an intervention might be received openly and in a responsive fashion by the dean. Such interventions require a good deal of tact by wise faculty leaders but can open the channels of communication and establish better working relationships between the administrator and the faculty.

The dean disciplinary process. While it is always better to solve communication and relationship problems at the lowest level—that is, between faculty and the dean—it may be necessary for faculty to take their concerns and complaints to the dean's boss. A provost or even president will no doubt be aware of conflicts and concerns regarding a dean's performance and personal failings. That knowledge may have come from the dean themselves. If so, it will emphasize the perceptions of the dean as to what the problems are and why they exist in this environment. Sometimes, when the dean is truly a disaster, faculty must take the initiative to seek help from those at the top of the organization.

The dean selection process. If the faculty have suffered under the reign of a bad dean, they might want to look at the process that led to such a poor choice for this leadership position. Doing so might not solve the present dilemma, but it will provide an opportunity for reflection on the criteria in place for hiring the dean. Were there red flags that the search committee should have seen? What can be learned from the unfortunate decision to hire this good professor for a position that they are not handling well? What can be done to improve the selection process itself to prevent disasters in the future?

The great majority of academic deans come from the ranks of the professoriate. This is as it should be: Who is better suited to understand the pressures and priorities of the faculty? Who is more acquainted with the demands of teaching, scholarship, and service? But not all good professors make good deans. In fact, many of the best professors wisely choose to maintain their successful roles in the faculty, eschewing any suggestion that they cross over "to the dark side" of administration. In those rare cases when a good professor is chosen to be dean and falls short, institutions should do all they can to improve the dean's performance and the relationships with the faculty before making a change in leadership. But sometimes only a change can lance the boil on the academic epidermis.

Dean as Academic Leader

Because you are reading this, I can assume that you not only are interested in academics but also have an important role to play in leading your institution toward academic excellence. Colleges and universities have many deans these days, but my thoughts turn to the work of those deans who are charged with curriculum and instruction, academic policy, faculty development, and the intellectual life of the college. What can academic deans do to advance the intellectual life of students and faculty in their colleges and universities?

I ask this question in part because so many of the demands placed on academic deans these days make academic leadership less than the priority it should be. As I look at my own calendar, I see myriad meetings devoted to budget crises, plant management, enrollment, athletics, development, and so many other topics that seem only indirectly connected to the central work of the chief academic officer. While these are important concerns for an academic dean, they often illustrate Steven Covey's declaration that "the urgent drives out the important." So I remind myself—and you, dear colleague—that teaching and learning and the educational mission of our college are what our work must ultimately be about. What are some of the things that academic deans can do to keep academic leadership atop the priority list? Here are some suggestions to consider as you remind yourself what is really important in your work life.

Be a role model

As you heard in your childhood, values are caught, not taught. If you want faculty and students to think that academic values are truly important, you can get that message across by being a teacher and scholar yourself. After all, people see you as the symbol of the academic mission of the institution, and your activities should be consonant with that expectation. You have to make time to teach a course—I taught four last year, and it just about killed me—and you have to force yourself to write for professional publication. But these activities do more to communicate your commitment to the academic life than almost anything else you can do.

Be a presence in the classroom

Even if you cannot continue to teach your own courses, you can be a guest lecturer for other professors. Beyond that, you can be an interested visitor (not just an evaluator) who stops by classrooms for brief visits. Once your faculty colleagues know that your modus operandi is one of positive curiosity about what is going on in classrooms, you can become a welcome sojourner in the academic vineyard. Brief conversations or even notes afterward that show appreciation for what you learned, rather than evaluative statements to "help" the teacher, can communicate your healthy interest in instruction.

Promote academic activities

This category might include your enthusiastic support for faculty forums, brown-bag lunches, faculty teaching seminars, visits with consultants on special academic topics, participation in student and faculty academic workshops, and other educational activities that feature your commitment to academic excellence outside the classroom as well as inside. Academic deans who take the time to send notes of congratulation or appreciation to students who have won scholarships, faculty who have had publications or received awards, and fellow administrators who have made contributions to the intellectual life of the college can claim to be academic boosters. You can make it your business to applaud any academic achievement that comes to your attention.

Provide resources

This means arguing for a budget that allows you to support special academic projects, student or faculty travel to academic conferences, academic award ceremonies, and a faculty library shelf devoted to academic issues. I try to provide such resources within our always limited budgets and am particularly pleased with the "professors' reading shelf." This shelf in the library includes a variety of practical books on college teaching, student motivation, testing and evaluation practices, and technology in the classroom. Academic deans need to produce visible commitments to the improvement of curriculum and instruction in their institutions if they are not to become mere bureaucrats.

While the increasing bureaucratic demands on academic deans threaten to drive out the important academic priorities to satisfy the urgent administrative demands of the day, academic leaders remind themselves that if they don't put academics first, they can hardly expect faculty and students to do so either. Sometimes you just have to take a deep breath and step back from the demands of the day to remind yourself why you got into this business in the first place. Remind yourself that teaching and learning are what it's all about and that the joy of deaning is to keep that priority alive and well.

Dean as Delegator

I don't know about you, but I always feel as though delegation is one of those practices that deans need to do better. I speak from sad personal experience. As dean (and now as provost), it seems my lot is to get delegated to—from above *and* below. Is that the price of middle management? Am I the exception? Where do I go wrong? Let's think about the dean as delegator.

The delegation dynamic

Delegation is one of those important management principles—operating both formally and informally—that good deans master.

Formally, administrators have certain duties and responsibilities that are outlined in job descriptions and handbooks. Much of the dynamic in the administration of a college is driven by assignment of tasks in accordance with these specified duties, a matter of deciding "whose job is this?" Transcript work goes to the registrar; dorm debates are settled by the director of housing; faculty conflicts are addressed by academic deans. Wise deans are careful about respecting formal duty parameters and decision-making processes. If they are not, they will breed the very conflict and confusion their job requires them to control.

Simply knowing whose job it is to do what—and respecting those assignments—promotes a healthy climate characterized by order, clarity, efficiency, good communication, and consistency.

The dean who delegates inconsistently, is confused about formal responsibilities of faculty and staff, or is inclined to give jobs to the hardest worker or nearest employee, feeds the bureaupathology of ineffective administration. This is a recipe for delegation for dysfunction.

Informally, deans have many opportunities to delegate duties, tasks, and assignments. Here is where superior deans distinguish themselves from average deans. Informal delegation opportunities often arise spontaneously:

in a conversation or departmental meeting or at a problem-solving conference. Will faculty respond to your suggestions, requests, and hints? Can you seize the moment by asking a fellow administrator to help you (and the college) complete a project? Do your friendship, high expectations, and enthusiasm invite cooperation and participation in meeting administrative objectives?

Administration at its best is simply getting work done through other people. Consequently, informal (as well as formal) delegation is what deaning is all about. True? There are no leaders without followers; delegation is the art of developing followership.

The delegation dilemma

To overcome my own delegation dilemmas, I have developed a few simple rules of deanly conduct that remind me how to be the delegator rather than the delegatee. Here they are for your consideration:

Delegate to relocate. As I look at the piles of paper in my office and examine my long to-do list, I try to prune and prioritize my projects by asking myself: Whose job is this anyway? Who can do it better than I can? Can I relocate this project—formally or informally—to someone else's less crowded plate?

Delegate to percolate. When my creative juices are not flowing and my administrative well runs dry, I ask myself: Is there a person or committee better able than I to see new solutions and more effective options for this problem? Where can I delegate this issue for brainstorming or rethinking so that consensus solutions might bubble up to the surface?

Delegate to elevate. Because I tend to see every decision and every project as *my* prerogative, I ask myself: Whose expertise and talents can I call on and promote by delegating responsibility in this instance? How can I do this as reward, not punishment, and how do I make this an opportunity more than an obligation?

Delegate, delegate, delegate

Some deans do not delegate because they do not want to lose control; some because they think they make better decisions than anyone else; some because they think delegation takes too much time; and some because they are reluctant to ask for help or fear their request will be rejected. All those things may be true; all delegation involves risk. But if you believe (as I do) that the dean's job is to get the job done through other people, then you should master the fine art of delegation.

How might you do that? For me there are some commonsense steps that keep me focused on better delegation practices:

Remember the rule. Administration is getting objectives of the college met through other people. Deans do not have the time or talent to accomplish everything that needs to be accomplished. We need other people—and should never forget that truth.

Resist the micromanager's fatal fall: endless meddling. Once you have delegated a task, provide support and a timeline—but stay out of the way. Micromanagers inevitably undermine the confidence of others and stunt their growth as decision-makers.

Review your delegation decisions. Were they *good* risks? Were they the *right* choices? Did they produce the *best* results?

What have *you* learned about delegation that other deans should know?

Faculty Morale: A Dean's Duty?

During my years as an academic dean at an independent liberal arts college, I often pondered the quixotic quality of "faculty morale." What is it? How do you measure it? Are there ways to improve it? Indeed, I was asked by the president and board chair, "How is morale among the professors, Tom?" I would try to look wise as I replied: "Remember the rule—faculty morale is *always* at an all-time low." But I know that answer was inadequate. Here is what 30-plus years as an academic leader have taught me about faculty morale.

What is faculty morale?

Beats me. I think the term is a code word that conveniently conveys one professor's perception, which they tend to project on the faculty in general. But as Mark Twain once commented, "No generalization is worth a damn —including this one." Often this code is used as a sort of faculty weather report, and like many weather reports, it gets more play when a storm is brewing. But just as the weather may be bad somewhere, elsewhere the sun is shining. The same shift in student enrollments that hurts morale in the physics department helps morale in the business department: it's an ill wind that blows no good. Call faculty morale the highly subjective individual and collective perception faculty have about the weather in their part of the academic world. Some might call it a "happiness reading."

How do we measure faculty morale?

Another perplexing problem. Because morale varies from time to time and from place to place within each institution, it is difficult to assess. Faculty don't usually like to claim high morale, because doing so takes the pressure off the dean to satisfy whatever need is current, from a new computer to better office accommodations to a lower course load to the ever-present better salary. The dean has to keep an ear close to the ground while not overreacting to faculty complaints. Sometimes deans can measure morale on campus against benchmark surveys and studies.

For example, *The American College Teacher*, a recent survey of 33,785 faculty members at 378 colleges, reports that faculty are getting older, older faculty feel more stress from technology than younger faculty, faculty in general are satisfied with their jobs (75 percent, up from 69 percent in 1989), and nearly 50 percent of them are happy with salaries but that almost 34 percent have thought about leaving campus life in the last two years. And only 58 percent were satisfied with their relationships with administrators. Such findings give deans benchmark temperature readings on various aspects of faculty life that affect morale.

Are there ways to improve faculty morale?

Certainly. As elusive and indefinable as the concept is, good academic leaders find ways to optimize faculty morale or they perish. It is imperative for academic leaders to have in place an action plan explicitly established to promote optimum faculty morale. Of course, that includes efforts to improve salary and working conditions, but the extensive research on faculty job satisfaction and morale makes it clear that the professoriate, more than most professions, is motivated by qualitative factors and workplace considerations: autonomy, achievement, respect, responsibility, freedom, collegiality, and support for creative research and teaching. A dean's duty is to understand those motivations and to support institutional efforts to respond to them.

An action agenda for deans

The dean who sees faculty morale as a duty—indeed, a priority—will design strategies to promote a culture that nurtures high faculty morale. This requires more than quick fixes and Band-Aids, more than recognition and rewards, more than friendly pats on the back. Deans should go beyond faculty development programs—faculty usually resent being "developed"— to think in terms of *faculty vitality*.

Developing an action agenda requires administrators to take some risks and expect some recrimination. As the saying goes, "No good dean goes unpunished." It is easier to assume the stance one of my colleagues does when he proudly calls himself "Dr. No": no to new ideas, no to creative research, no to funding unproven teaching experiments.

I rather like the persona of another colleague who calls herself "the Dean of Exceptions." She is willing to say yes, even when that decision may break precedent or rule—if a yes advances faculty morale. The risks, of course, include failed experiments, grumbling about "favoritism," and questions about "what have you done for me lately?"

Good deans are willing to take these lumps in the interest of a proactive action agenda to promote faculty vitality.

In an excellent publication from the Council of Independent Colleges (CIC) entitled *A Good Place to Work* (1991), Austin, Rice, and Splete evaluate the research on faculty morale and identify a host of factors that characterize vitality at selected "high-morale colleges." A dean might well begin with suggestions from this study.

The CIC study found morale to be highest at independent liberal arts colleges where there was
- a strong sense of community and distinctive organizational culture;
- a clear understanding of and agreement with institutional goals, values, traditions, celebrations, and rituals;
- a wide definition of faculty scholarship with rewards not limited to published research;
- an effort to promote participatory leadership;
- an intentional focus on teaching and students;
- a commitment to momentum (growth, progress, and excellence);
- an emphasis on internal collaboration rather than competition, supported by collegiality and a balance of intrinsic and extrinsic rewards; and
- a strong tie with the surrounding community.

Can deans and other academic leaders find ways to advance these institutional qualities? Of course. The CIC project includes "The Academic Workplace Audit," an instrument that can help deans assess faculty morale in their own institutions and establish a more specific action agenda to improve faculty vitality: not a bad place to begin establishing a high-morale faculty.

In such a climate we might also find more "high-morale deans," deans who do not lose their faculties. Deans cannot make faculty happy (perhaps because, as Abraham Lincoln observed, "most people are about as happy as they make up their minds to be"), but they do have a duty to support and serve faculty goals and ambitions that also advance the institutional mission. Making judgments about such personal and college congruence of goals takes both wisdom and courage; however, such judgments and commitments help create the kind of climate in which faculty vitality and high morale are natural by-products. To do less is to miss deaning's greatest opportunity—and greatest satisfaction.

Leading the Faculty: A Dean's Definition

Leadership. Every academic dean is charged to lead the faculty—like herding cats, we sometimes say—in such areas as curriculum reform, instructional effectiveness, computer literacy (and beyond), and governance. Deans are, by definition, leaders. They rise (some faculty say fall) to their administrative positions because they aspire to leadership—perhaps lured by wildly exaggerated expectations of power and fame—and because they demonstrate leadership ability. What *is* that ability? How is it manifest in the role and work of the dean? Are there lessons in leadership that prescribe useful behaviors for other deans and middle managers?

The book on leadership

There is no shortage of books on leadership. Indeed, Amazon will gladly ship you any one of over 5,000 current titles on this engaging topic. Among the top 50 on its best-seller list are such titles as *The 3 Keys to Empowerment* (Ken Blanchard), *7 Secrets of Exceptional Leadership* (Christopher Hegerty and Philip Nelson), *The 9 Natural Laws of Leadership* (Warren Blank), *10 Steps to Empowerment* (Diane Tracy), *The 21 Irrefutable Laws of Leadership* (John Maxwell), *30 Days to Confident Leadership* (Bobb Biehl), and *40 Tools for Cross-Functional Teams.* Actually, the numbers keep escalating to *1,001 Ways to Energize Employees* (Bob Nelson) and *The 2,000 Percent Solution* (Donald Mitchell, Carol Coles, and Robert Metz).

My own preferences run toward more seasoned texts, including those by Tom Peters (*The Pursuit of Wow!*), Stephen Covey (*Principle-Centered Leadership*), Warren Bennis (*On Becoming a Leader*), James Kouzes and Barry Posner (*The Leadership Challenge*), and Max De Pree (*Leadership Is an Art*). Every expert on leadership has a particular point of view and a persuasive prescription for empowering (a term in vogue), transforming, or inspiring those of us—including deans—in positions of leadership. Whether you aspire to excellence or total quality, you will find advice aplenty in your bookstore.

A personal perspective

While I have read a lot, have written a little, and still teach a graduate course on the challenges in leadership in education, I think experience has been my best teacher. One learns as much from mistakes as from successes, of course, but the cardinal rule for deans should be to *reflect on actions and consequences* to see what lessons lie therein. I say that in part because leadership, especially in the unique arena of the academy, is too human and idiosyncratic an enterprise to be totally susceptible to rule and prescription. Faculty "cats" require a different brand of leadership than might be found in other organizations. The best deans I have seen in action seem to have found that happy balance of decisiveness and flexibility necessary to lead with confidence, compassion, and competency. How do they do it?

With some caution, I suggest my own numbered principles for success, a mere five aphorisms that I state as pithily as possible for easy recall. These deceptively simple rules for deaning cut across most theories—from situational to servant leadership—but ultimately are rooted in Warren Bennis's claim in *On Becoming a Leader* that "at bottom, becoming a leader is synonymous with becoming yourself" (p. 9). That is to say, leadership is a process of human development and self-fulfillment. A dean's definition depends, most of all, on the dean.

Five leadership aphorisms for deans

1. Read to lead

No one guru, theory, or book has all the answers. (That may be why Amazon has a growing list of books on leadership.) But books and publications like *Academic Leader, Administrator*, and others are rich sources of research, theory, and practice that no good dean should neglect. Deans can expand their experience vicariously by reading about the success and failures of leaders from Jesus (*Transforming Leadership* by Leighton Ford) to college basketball coach Dean Smith (*12 Leadership Principles of Dean Smith* by David Chadwick).

2. Drive to arrive

Leaders must themselves be led by a calling—a vocation—that puts them in front. That drive may be in low gear or high (beware of overdrive), calm and focused, or creative and flamboyant. If the dean lacks the energy and work ethic it takes to steer the faculty in a direction that points to a better college and better educational experience for students, the institution will merely drift into the future. Deans, then, need not only energy but also goals for themselves and the faculty they lead. Deans are likely to be most successful when they derive their goals from the collective will and vision of the faculty itself, leading the faculty in a helpful, nourishing fashion without taking credit for successes. Deans are the drivers, not the passengers, in the educational van.

3. Inspire their desire

Faculty are an independent lot, guided by personal research interests and working within (too often, it seems) balkanized department structures that may suffer from intellectual hardening of the arteries. Good deans know how to design and articulate a vision that captures the imagination and commitment of even the most hardened and cynical in the professoriate. This takes time and talent—to present well-reasoned proposals and to convince faculty that certain goals are worth working toward. The most effective deans know how to connect institutional goals to the interests and motivation of the faculty. The ability to inspire is what separates leaders from managers.

4. Walk your talk

This old aphorism captures the essence of deaning. In the academy, leadership is earned, and it depends less on positional authority than on personal authenticity. If deans expect faculty to be effective teachers, deans themselves must be regarded as exemplary teachers; so it is with research and publication, advising, committee work, and community service. Further, if deans expect faculty to be team oriented, committed to institutional priorities, and open to change, they should themselves be the best examples of such values and practices on campus. Talk is cheap. The old virtues—honesty, fairness, and integrity—still count for those who would garner the support of faculty.

5. Deserve to serve

Believe it or not, some deans forget that their primary duty is to serve—faculty, students, boards, and the institution. The term *administrator* derives from the Latin word *ministrare* (to serve). In *Servant Leadership*, Robert K. Greenleaf explores this useful concept, observing that "among those now in titular positions in institutions both large and small are some who would find greater joy in their lives if they raised the servant aspect of their leadership and built more serving institutions" (p. 5) Serving means listening with the "third ear," identifying and tapping into faculty talents and needs, and building a community of consensus—tough service indeed. In a word, serving means putting the welfare of others ahead of one's own. Deans who can do that deserve to serve.

A dean's definition

The five concepts of leadership above suggest that leading a college faculty is less a matter of management skill or even great wisdom, useful as these may be, than of personal power granted by the faculty to the dean. Leading can be learned: to lead, a dean must learn to listen and to serve. As John Heider's *The Tao of Leadership* translates Lao Tzu's ancient and timeless insights into leaders: "Their leadership did not rest on techniques or on theatrics but on silence and their ability to pay attention. . . . They could clarify events for others because they had done it for themselves" (p. 29). And "the leader teaches more through being than through doing" (p. 45).

As any dean will tell you, leading the faculty is a difficult and demanding responsibility. My five definitional concepts are only a start on a dean's self-definition of leadership. (Other useful aphorisms might include "delegate to elevate," "be humble when you stumble," and "know when to go.") Reflect on the consequences of your leadership behavior and the ways your personal qualities define your leadership style. Remember, as Bennis says, that becoming a leader is really just a matter of becoming yourself.

2

The New Dean's Toolbox

So you're a new dean, charged with the care and feeding of many faculty and staff (think of all the directors who have become ubiquitous in higher education institutions in recent years!) as well as large numbers of students (and their helicopter parents) now under your "control." The world you now occupy in the groves of academe may be a familiar one, whether you have occupied a similar position in another institution or have labored in the very same one you are expected to lead with joy and enthusiasm as you implement your new vision, new policies, and new expectations for those now in your care. Good luck with that, as Dr. Phil often says. You really can succeed, of course, but this might be a good time to review your dean's toolbox to see what instruments are already there—or might be needed—for the tasks ahead.

A hammer. Of course, no toolbox is complete without this most essential instrument. Your leadership position requires the ability to come down hard when quick, firm action is essential. Every dean must be able to communicate some decisions forcefully, with no room for ambiguity or contrary point of view. Naturally, there will have been much lead-up, in most cases, to provide for debate and contrary arguments, but sometimes you must assert your "police role" to ensure final debate resolution. As Abraham Maslow famously remarked, however, "If your only tool is a hammer, you tend to see every problem as a nail." The key to successful deaning often lies in the dean's patience and discretion in using the "administrator's hammer" as a last resort. Do you know when, where, and on whom to use this essential tool?

A saw. Every dean will face decisions that result in cutting someone or some policy loose from firm moorings in the institution. These painful decisions for all concerned test the dean's ability to be a good communicator who can articulate why the cut is necessary so that everyone understands. An arbitrary dean—who may also be viewed as a micromanager—may win in the short run, but over time the saw gets dull, and sympathy for the dean dissipates. As with the hammer, one must use the saw sparingly and only when logic and reliable information fully justify one's decision. Can't afford to support a costly faculty trip that has little value for the institution? Have to let an employee go because of poor performance? Need to let a student leave your place for greener pastures where they might be more successful? Use the saw, and do not leave any jagged edges if you can help it.

Sandpaper. The first two tools can leave rough spots on the academic epidermis. Effective deans know how to administer policies and practices that soften the impact and smooth rough edges, for all concerned, of negative decisions left by hammer and saw. Yes, a dean is sometimes the institutional police force but also sometimes the pastor who provides wise counsel and a sympathetic ear. Are you a good listener who can hear the real message in a tirade or lament? Do you listen with what Eastern philosophers call "the third ear"? We sometimes say about teaching that students don't care what you know until they know that you care. The same is true for administrators. How do you pour oil on troubled waters? Your ability to be a healer and one who makes the rough spots smooth is a real test of your leadership; no toolbox is complete without sandpaper.

A drill. "Drilling down" has been a staple of administrative jargon in recent years and addresses the need to go below the surface of an issue or problem. In the rush of daily duties, deans sometimes just need to take a deep breath and think more deeply about how to deal with a problem student, staff member, or professor. Have you done enough research? Have you talked to enough (and the right) people? Do you have alternative possibilities and options that you have not seriously considered? Get out the drill! Quick decisions and actions may make you seem like an efficient and decisive dean, but at what cost? Perhaps one more day or one more conversation will result in a better decision or action—and will be well worth your patient drilling.

Tape. A final item for your dean's toolbox is a roll of strong tape. You will often encounter broken promises, unhinged personnel, disconnected policies, and practices that need mending. The administrator's tape can help reconnect those things in your dean's duties that badly need your skillful application of this essential tool. Are students at odds with their professors? Is a department fractured by rivalries and jealousies? Are two of your directors not on the same page when it comes to handling the disputes or disagreements of other personnel? This is the time to get out the tape and bind the broken parts! How do you do that? It may require you to use some of the other tools above— but always with the goal of unifying where there is disunity and healing where there are broken bones. Part of your role as dean is to do your best to have everyone working harmoniously toward common purposes: help where you can, counsel where you must, and take firm action if that is essential to put things back together the way they need to be for the health and wholeness of the enterprise you lead.

There are other tools for your toolbox, of course, and you might consider what else you might want to have ready as you begin dealing with the exciting challenges of a new deanship.

More Tools for the New Dean's Toolbox

The previous essay became the basis of a session I led for new deans at the very first Magna Leadership in Higher Education Conference held in Atlanta in the fall of 2016 as Hurricane Matthew whipped up its destructive winds on the East Coast. The conference and my session were well received. In my session, I asked the new deans to suggest additional tools they thought the toolbox should include. They had some very good ideas, including these below:

A flashlight. In every institution, there are dark corners that an alert dean should illuminate lest they encounter rough surprises from things that go bump in the night. Sometimes these are the institutional skeletons in the closet or some of the submerged resentments and conflicts that have been swept under the rug but remain sore spots on the academic epidermis. Solving the resulting dilemma requires the bright light of disclosure so that the dean can address the problems with both eyes open. What one sees on the surface is often obscured by the dark rooms in the cellar below. Do you know everything you need to know and understand when a dilemma reaches your office?

Measuring tape. The old saying every carpenter and seamstress knows is "measure twice and cut once." How long has a problem been festering? How deep does it go? Do not be too hasty to make a decision now that you may regret later and could have avoided had you only measured twice. Knowing the dimensions of an issue—its height and depth—is the first step in a process requiring thoughtful and accurate measuring before taking your scissors to the fabric. In your busy administrative world, remember that other old saying: haste makes waste. Take the time required to measure twice (or even more) so that you avoid a rushed decision. Have you taken accurate readings of all aspects of the issue?

A C-clamp. This is a tool you will use only in rare cases where you know that the solution to a conflict between, say, two faculty members can be achieved only by the warring parties themselves. The problem is they are so invested in contrary positions that compromise and creative solutions seem unlikely—even impossible. Your approach need not be a win-lose decision by you (which the parties in conflict may well view as a lose-lose solution), but you can insist that the combatants come together to work out a solution to which both can live. Here is where you bring in the C-clamp. It requires forcing the two together and holding them in place until they reach a consensus. You might not want to leave them alone together in a locked room (!), but do keep them in a productive conversation. Do you see places where a C-clamp might be your best tool?

A balance. This helpful instrument is somewhat like the measuring tape—but usually comes into play during and after a dilemma has been addressed by the dean. As poet Robert Bridges put it in *The Testament of Beauty* (1929): "Our stability is but balance and wise conduct lies in masterful administration of the unforeseen." Administering unseen developments is part of a dean's difficult role in the institution; the balance gives you a tool to use when you answer questions like Was my decision fair? *Was my response properly measured and temperate? and Will this solution stay in place rather than tilting out of control later?* Deans often have to find their own balance points between their roles as pastor and policeman and between their obligations to treat faculty equally and the need to take differences into account. A dean who is perceived to play favorites is a danger to the institutional balance you are asked to honor and preserve. How balanced are your decisions?

WD-40. While it took the inventors of this useful spray 40 attempts to get it right, a dean can use it right away to eliminate some of the squeaks and groans from the many individuals reporting to you. Sometimes a complainer needs only the lubrication of your gentle and sympathetic voice. Do you listen patiently to a program director's lament or a staff member's criticism of a decision affecting their work? A dean who listens carefully to discern what is really behind an issue, the cause of the conflict or complaint that has disrupted the machinery in the communication process, may well be able to lubricate the offending joints. Reframing a complaint in a way that lets the aggrieved person know you really do understand the issue may be all that is required to eliminate the friction. You want your institution or given unit to work like a well-oiled machine! A smooth-running administrative unit requires judicious leadership from a dean who knows just where to apply WD-40. Do you have a can of this lubricant in your toolbox?

Academic leaders have many challenges because they are so often caught betwixt and between competing pressures and responsibilities. It will not always be easy as you try to administer the unforeseen. But if you have a well-stocked personal toolbox, you may find the job more satisfying and successful than you could have imagined. Your new dean colleagues and I have given you a starter kit, your new dean's toolbox, as you take on the exciting work in the groves of academe. Can you think of other tools you might want to have?

The Art of Diplomacy

Diplomat—"someone who can tell you to go to hell in such a way that you begin to look forward to the trip." Well, dean colleague, how good of a diplomat are you? The best deans I know have honed their diplomatic skills to a fine art. Let's talk about diplomacy as one of those essential ingredients in a dean's arsenal of human relations skills. After all, we academic leaders are in the people business, working with highly intelligent faculty, serving in loosely coupled organizational systems, and succeeding not so much by institutionalized authority as by our ability to persuade.

Why be a diplomat?

Deans are quintessential middle managers. Their jobs require them to be superior communicators: between themselves and the president or provost, among warring faculty members or departments, and to virtually everyone inside and outside the college. Middle managers as communicators simply must know how to defuse conflict, bring different constituencies together, explain and sell policy—often to those who feel aggrieved, abused, or unfairly treated—and promote the peace. A dean who believes that unilateral decrees and power politics will achieve such ends should think again.

Deans need to know how to negotiate between and among a dizzying array of power centers: the trustees, president, provost or vice president for academic affairs, faculty senate or union, donors, governmental agencies, accrediting bodies, parents, and students. We live in an age when grievances are quickly asserted, rights are readily claimed, and everyone wants to go to the top for solutions to problems, real or imagined. When deans promote diplomatic solutions (usually called "win-win" in the parlance of organizational gurus), they serve their colleges *and* constituents well. The consequence is less friction, smoother administrative operations, more productive work, better harmony, higher morale, stronger college reputation, more effective public relations, and less noise and negativity. Have I persuaded you yet?

Diplomacy principles

My guess is that you already embrace the notion that good deans should be good diplomats. The more challenging quest is to become even more diplomatic than you already are. Toward that end, consider these principles of diplomacy. Check your own views and actions against them as a guide to better deaning:

Identify real interests and needs. Almost all win-win solutions to conflicts require the brokering of interests and needs by the diplomat. Because individuals (or whole departments) sometimes disguise their real interests and actual needs—putting forth, instead, a nobler, more principled rationale for what they want—the diplomatic dean must listen carefully to discern what is really at issue. Psychologist William Glasser in *Control Theory* says that all human behavior is motivated by one or more of four basic psychological needs: belonging, freedom, power, fun. Diplomats learn to listen with "the third ear" to discern the motive behind the rhetoric. Is your president *really* upset because of a perceived loss of power? Is an untenured faculty member *actually* protesting a lack of freedom? Is a failing student *fundamentally* seeking more fun or feeling ostracized by classmates? Only when the diplomat has identified root causes of problems will they be able to propose solutions that satisfy.

Develop patience. Deans are often impatient people. They have busy calendars, long to-do lists, and a penchant for action. But diplomats have learned that win-win solutions that last are not quickly achieved, especially when values are at issue. Think about the Middle East peace process when you get exasperated by the slow pace of your progress in conflict resolution on your campus. Patience is related in meaning to suffering (as in a doctor's patient), and most of us cannot abide pain. As a diplomat, however, a dean learns that some problems must be waited out. Avoid the "ready, fire, aim" approach of the impatient dean. (Wanting something *now*, Freud noted, is an immature impulse of childhood behavior.) If you need to become more patient, try these tips:

- Find tasks that bridge the frustration gap.
- Find patient colleagues to talk with.
- Schedule delays on your planner.

- Take action in some other area that might contribute to a faster solution in the area on hold.
- Remember: hasty solutions are often counterproductive.

Patient deans do not force unwise, ephemeral solutions but do nurture the processes of dialogue, debate, and decision-making.

Be flexible. Diplomatic deans keep their options open as they look for win-win solutions. They do not sell out on essential principles and core values, of course, but they have learned to negotiate in good faith and with imagination to solve thorny college conundrums. Flexible deans strive to find a creative consensus as opposed to a weak compromise.

Do you listen well? Are you patient? Can you be flexible? If so, you have what it takes to be a diplomatic dean.

The Power of Listening

Can you hear me? CAN YOU HEAR ME NOW? This familiar commercial for a phone service reminds us of the importance of hearing. For those of us who are aging administrators, hearing can be an ever-greater challenge. As the saying goes, old deans never die—they just lose their faculties. But more important than the faculty of hearing is the capacity of listening. The two are not the same.

One would think that anyone could be a good listener, but that (my experience tells me) is not the case in college administration. What keeps us from being better listeners? Here are a few possible barriers:

Self-protection. If we take the time to listen to someone, we might have to hear some unpleasant truths (or at least opinions) about ourselves. We might also have to rethink a decision or change an attitude or belief. I would rather not expose my vulnerabilities.

Self-deception. After all, we are in charge! It is up to us to make hard decisions, to communicate them to others, to defend the policies we are trying (against daunting odds) to implement. My power comes from telling, yelling, and selling.

Self-absorption. We are so busy. Our agendas are so full. Our needs are so compelling. Administration is all about us. Listening to others takes concentration and effort that we do not have time for. If they would just listen to *my* needs and desires!

Effective administrators know that there is real power in listening. This does not mean showing mere courtesy to one's colleagues and followers. How many administrators pretend to listen while, in reality, they are only waiting for their turn and are mentally rehearsing their next argument? Leading requires intense and honest listening, hearing with what has been called "the third ear." This extra ear listens for meaning, emotion, and values that are below the conversational surface.

In *The Tao of Leadership*, John Heider's modern translation and application of fifth century BC Chinese philosopher Lao Tzu's advice to ancient leaders, Lao says that "the wise leader stays in the background and facilitates other people's process. . . . Because the leader is open, an issue can be raised. . . . What is soft is strong. . . . The wise leader is quiet and reflective." Not bad advice for academic leaders today.

Are you a good listener? How is that third ear? Can you hear me now?

Academic Leader as Communicator in Chief

Those of us who have served our institutions as deans or provosts know that leadership requires many skills, some of which we bring to the job and some of which we develop in office. I think that the ability to communicate effectively is one that is always a work in progress—partly because it is so challenging and partly because it demands abilities that are not inherent in the leader's personality. Yes, we have budgets to manage, decisions to make, and innovations to pursue, but if we do not take seriously our roles as communicators in chief, we will likely not fare well in the many tasks that accompany our administrative responsibilities.

Sometimes our duties include making formal speeches to various groups: students, faculty, boards of trustees, and conferencegoers, to mention but a few. In these cases, the task requires having something worth saying and presenting our remarks in a coherent and concise fashion. Too many times, we may find ourselves off topic, meandering, and even rambling. Some sage—no doubt a dean somewhere—once noted that any speech, on any topic, to any audience, on any occasion can be made better simply by making it *shorter*: words to live by when we construct a formal presentation. In an *Academic Leader* article, titled "My Last Commencement Speech (p. 111)," I presented my own formula for this kind of formal presentation; of course, the formal speech itself requires effective delivery techniques if it is to serve its intended purpose. And those techniques include avoiding common speech errors of the kind we hear in virtually every news commentary we tune in to on television these days.

Common speech flaws

Here are some of the things you will hear from the expert pundits as they respond to a question from the moderator: "Well . . . you know . . . I mean . . . so . . . and . . . that said, I believe my answer would be . . ." By that point, the listener may be reaching for the remote! The dean or other academic leader may well fall into similar diversionary tactics while thinking of something substantive to say. This is a flaw less common in formal talks than in less formal settings—such as panel sessions, conferences with department chairs, and interviews with reporters—but effective speakers know how to focus quickly on a response or point of argument. Other flaws include mumbling (poor articulation), word choice (poor diction), and using a volume level that is too soft or too loud for the occasion (poor projection). In any event, the verbal part of the communication process offers many areas where we academic leaders can find something to improve in our own formal and informal speeches.

Nonverbal communication

Speech teachers tell us that effective communication relies more on nonverbal techniques than verbal ones. Perhaps the one area here that most of us could work on is listening. Listening is often the key to a productive conversation—even with a large audience where questions are sought and answered by the speaker. How well do you hear the *actual* point of a question or comment from a student or faculty member? Do you hear the unspoken message embedded in the verbal message? Can you read the body language so well that you know what the speaker is really trying to communicate? Is your eye contact just right—not piercing but still direct and receptive? In one-on-one conversations, have you developed active listening techniques advocated by such educator specialists as Thomas Gordon and William Glasser? These include simple things like a receptive posture and head nodding, "empathic grunting" ("hmmm . . . uh-huh . . . ah"), "door openers" ("tell me more about that"), and most importantly, paraphrasing responses before you respond to make sure you have heard exactly what has been the speaker's intended message. These listening techniques require practice to master and can be overused to the point where they seem phony—but that is where developed skill becomes critical.

I hope my communication has been clear and concise—no need to belabor points that are common knowledge for any academic leader. Even so, I suspect all of us can find some aspect of our communication talents to work on as we engage our many audiences in both formal and informal venues. Let me be so bold as to suggest that you find one or two in the discussion above to perfect. The challenge is to meld given techniques into one's own personal style and value system. Your academic world has plenty of opportunities to practice any of these skills in your role as communicator-in-chief.

Dean as Terminator

While I sometimes envy Arnold Schwarzenegger's ability to terminate the world's miscreants, today I have in mind the dean's responsibility to terminate employees. This is never as much fun as Arnold seems to have. As educators, deans are more comfortable with rescue efforts to help a struggling faculty member or mediocre administrator. There is great satisfaction in redeeming the lost but none at all in removing the hopeless. So what are your options when the only just course of action for an employee is termination?

Termination strategies

Here are a few of the most widely used approaches for the inevitable decanal dismissals:

The personal approach. When you employ this strategy, you use your human relations skills to communicate with an employee who needs to go. In this approach you are as sympathetic as is possible for a dean to be. As both counselor and pastor, you convey the difficult decision you have had to make, and you hope that the employee feels your pain. This approach works best with those with whom you have a good personal relationship, in spite of your judgment that their work simply does not measure up to acceptable standards.

The subtle approach. In some cases, you may decide to let the employee understand from hints and suggestions that they should consider another place of employment. Let the employee know that you will be happy to recommend them should a wonderful new opportunity emerge. Suggestions that the employee's skills do not match up as well in your college as they might somewhere else or hints that downsizing because of an enrollment downturn might affect the employee's position can sometimes be enough to create a self-initiated employee departure.

The legal approach. Deans must be supersensitive to the legal requirements for dismissal. This means making sure that you have followed all the rules and regulations of the institution and that you have documentation to substantiate "just cause" for dismissal. This is especially important if the employee is a tenured faculty member, and you best be fortified by your knowledge of state law, AAUP guidelines, faculty union agreements, and due process rights. You should also have a good working relationship with the institution's legal counsel and have the support of your administrative superiors.

The pressure approach. Another way an administrator can hasten an employee's departure is by keeping the employee in a pressure cooker and gradually turning up the heat. The dean keeps piling up the work and speeding up the deadlines. The employee may be asked to do the work of others in the department who have had the good sense to look elsewhere for employment. You can increase the pressure by assigning the worst teaching times, most onerous committees, and most tedious reports. Just as a pressure washer can flush out the rust and mold from your basement floor, so the pressure of too much work can flush out those who cannot handle the stress and strain of your workplace.

I do not necessarily recommend these approaches, but I have seen all of them in use at the college level by deans who are certain that the institution would be better if a given employee could be enticed, cajoled, or required to leave the dean's institution for better opportunities elsewhere.

A word to the wise

Much of a dean's work is personnel related. The fun part of the job is hiring exciting new people to inspire your students and support institutional needs. The better able we are to select top-flight teachers, administrators, and staff at the front end, the fewer times we need to deal with the unpleasant duty of termination. Once we hire good people, we need to encourage them, support them, train them, reward them, and tap into their strengths to make the institution a dynamic and positive place for everyone.

That's how most of us should spend most of our time. The better we are at making hires and developing employees, the better we fulfill our primary responsibility as administrators.

But sometimes we do not make the right choice at the front end, do not tap into the creative talents of the employee, and in the end have no alternative but to find an effective way to separate the employee from the institution. The dean as terminator cannot avoid this responsibility, including knowing how best to dismiss that occasional bad employee. We should always remember that in such cases we who hire also bear some of the responsibility for the inadequacy of the one we must fire.

Decisive Deaning

Do you ever ask faculty to evaluate you? (I mean in the formal way of a questionnaire; they will *always* evaluate you). My institution does not require that of academic administrators, but I submit myself to faculty review every so often to find out what the professoriate thinks about my style and performance. Surveys are collected and summarized by the president's assistant and sent to me with statistics and typed comments. Reviewing the results is a worthwhile if sometimes painful exercise.

Just as faculty respond to results of student evaluations of instruction, I gravitate toward the narrative comments in the sections on strengths and weaknesses. My last evaluation brought forth excessive commendations, far exceeding my self-assessment, for such strengths as these:

- "Tom is very supportive, is readily available, and listens. He works hard at being fair to all conflicting parties."
- "Dr. McDaniel makes an effort to lead meetings in a fair and balanced manner, seeking input from all parties and helping the meeting move toward a resolution. He is a good listener; he is fair in his decision-making."
- "Trustworthy, positive, ethical, receptive. Does his best to help resolve problems brought to him. Excellent administrative 'people skills.'"
- "His fairness, his wit, and his problem-solving skills."
- "Tom's ability to harmonize and yet be able to move forward."
- "He is a great facilitator, and he has a gift for working with diverse constituencies without offending."

Gracious, what a paragon of provostial perfection! Of course, I bask in the radiance of such praise—and hope my faculty have not seen my recent column on how to apply Machiavelli to deaning.

But then, I turn to the weaknesses and see evaluative statements like the following:

- "Perhaps because of the above traits (personable, approachable person who gets along with everyone, capable) this prevents him from taking 'a stand' on issues."
- "Tom needs to tell 'some faculty members' to 'straighten up and fly right' and not always be so diplomatic."
- "Often I wish he would be more forceful. I often want decisions to be made more quickly and of course in my favor."
- "Tom's strength of seeking consensus can be offset by a slowness in making decisions."
- "Appears too often to have great difficulty making decisions."

Goodness, what an exemplar of enervating inefficiency! Naturally, I cringe and am wounded by such criticism. Perhaps, as one faculty member put it, my strengths are also my weaknesses. Am I *decisive* enough? I don't know; I can't make up my mind about that criticism. While some praise me for being fair, patient, and a good listener who builds consensus, others looking at the same qualities want me to take stands, take action (and "take names and kick butt," as one put it).

Pastor or policeman?

When it comes to decision-making, deans must often choose between listening and counseling on the one hand and action on the other. Of course, the best deans listen well and then take the exact actions the situation requires. Most deans, however, lean in one direction or the other as preferred styles of deaning.

Dean as pastor

Some deans are thoughtful, deliberative, and patient—that is to say, pastor-like in their approach to decision-making. They seek first to understand, then to be understood (as Stephen Covey puts it). They may well score high on the "Feeling" scale of the Myers-Briggs Type Indicator and may tend toward the introvert dimension (I am a classic INFJ) of this the most widely used psychological inventory in the world. Such deans may have had training and experience as counselors. Their inclination is to clarify issues, identify options, and build consensus; they like to see decisions emerge from the group or be reached by individuals who are most affected by the decision.

Dean as policeman

Other deans, however, are instinctive, alert, and astute—quick to see the choices in a situation and quick to resolve it with a firm, no-nonsense decision. That is, some deans are police-like in their approach to deaning. After all, they are in charge, have authority, and know that definitive decisions are often required to keep problems from escalating. They will often gladly trade diplomacy for the respect a leader can win with efficient decisions. Deans who resemble police are often appreciated for their ability as troubleshooters; they may tend toward the "Thinking" and "Extrovert" preferences on the Myers Briggs. Such deans—classic ESTJs—like making decisions for themselves and others, letting the chips fall where they may.

So, deans out there in academe, what's your preference? Can you justify one decision-making style over the other? Is there a happy medium? Do you have criteria for when to behave as pastor or policeman? (This choice suggests situational leadership.) Or is this a false dichotomy? You know which way I lean as a general rule or preferred style. How about you?

Devilish Deaning: WWMD?

My son the political philosopher, who works under a devilish dean at a here-unnamed state university, assures me that Stanley Bing's new book, *What Would Machiavelli Do?*, misses the essence of the great political thinker's advice to rulers. But the idea—and the image of deans buying wristbands inscribed with "WWMD?"—got me thinking about my administrative colleagues out there in academia. That new book attempts to draw lessons from *The Prince* (1513) for modern corporate leaders. (That Bing's subtitle is *The Ends Justify the Meanness* should warn you it is tongue-in-cheek satire.) Because colleges and universities increasingly resemble corporations, we might look to such current applications of Machiavelli's rules for advice about successful political action. If there are no politics to worry about on your campus, feel free to stop reading now.

Sometimes I think deaning is nothing but politics—usually in the best sense of that term but not always. Recall this axiom: academic politics are so vicious because the stakes are so low. But for those in the academy, the stakes are anything but low. Promotion, tenure, project funding, travel budgets, departmental and committee chairmanships—all are determined by political processes, and deans are often thrust (or thrust themselves) right into the middle of political debates, diatribes, and dynamics.

What Machiavelli wanted to do was explain politics and power in terms of human nature. That's where we come in. Although his true purpose is obscure, conflicting, and complex, he offered to those who lead institutions a practical and down-to-earth set of principles. How might rulers secure the stability of their institutions? That's a practical question, said Machiavelli, not a matter of grand ideals, pious pronouncements, or the private morality of the leader. Leadership depends on getting followers to comply with the leader's will; they will do so if the leader acts in accord with their human nature.

Here, then, are a few Machiavellian ideas for you devilish deans who think your job includes strong political leadership to secure peace and order in your institution:

Use selfish human nature to accomplish your noble ends. Machiavelli broke from the Greek's classical virtues and the medieval church's religious values to suggest that leadership should be guided not by morality or piety but by an understanding of human motives. Deans, then, might remember that material rewards may be more important than appeals to faculty to serve the common good or sacrifice for the sake of pure learning.

Learn from the fox and the lion. Bing writes, "Skillful use of paranoia paired with a warlike stance is the bedrock upon which all Machiavellian rulership is based." Machiavelli suggests that at times leaders must use strength to punish foes and cunning to fool them. The wise ruler keeps as a top priority the need to discipline the troops, control the action, win the war. Force and trickery are legitimate tools in academic battle.

Prefer to be more feared than loved. This is a fundamental concept in Machiavelli's approach to leadership. He and Bing say that leaders should make enemies and then use power to punish them as examples of power in practice. Bing says, "I find the best time to attack people is very early in the morning . . . or at the end of afternoon when they think the worst is behind them." It is impossible to run a Machiavellian operation without firing people. Keep your faculty thinking about that.

Negotiate. Machiavelli figured out that—base human nature being what it is—people will act for the common good only if it is also in their private interest. The utilitarian principle of reciprocity is one a skillful dean should use to "sell" (Machiavelli was never above the fine art of manipulation) a particular program or idea. Always answer a faculty member's unasked but always present question: What's in it for me?

Put your power to work. At bottom, *The Prince* is a cookbook on power. Power, Machiavelli argued, is a positive concept that helps leaders establish orderly organizations where peace and stability promote the self-interests of both ruler and ruled. Power should be used to force, convince, manipulate, and persuade followers to do those things the ruler knows to be essential for the welfare of all—especially the ruler. And if the ends justify the meanness, so be it.

So tell me: Are you mean enough? Do you know how to negotiate to capitalize on reciprocal self-interest? Can you give up your need to be loved? Where would you draw the line—Trickery? Screaming? Public ridicule?

Distorted Deaning

In a fascinating mental fitness guide titled *Managing Your Mind*, Gillian Butler and Tony Hope ask us to consider how "crooked thinking" can give us a distorted vision of the world. Drawing on theories of cognitive therapy, they identify 13 varieties of inaccurate, biased, and negative thinking patterns that contribute to bad feelings and a misplaced sense of inadequacy.

I always thought of myself as an upbeat, positive, win-win kind of thinker as I dealt with all the problems facing a college administrator. But I found myself indicted by several of the crooked thinking habits Butler and Hope present. Yes, even I have been guilty of "distorted deaning." Check yourself on the survey of unwarranted and unproductive tendencies (the examples are mine) that keep us from seeing our problems clearly:

Catastrophizing. If something goes wrong, it will be a disaster. Example: "If the chair of the English department resigns, our new writing program is down the tubes."

Overgeneralizing. If something happened once, it will surely happen again. Example: "Whenever the president asks my opinion, I never give one he likes."

Exaggerating. Giving negative events too much weight. Example: "Any fool could get this computer to boot up."

Discounting the positive. If something good results from your actions, it can't amount to much. Example: "I was just plain lucky that the curriculum committee took my recommendation."

Mind reading. Believing you know what others are thinking. Example: "Four faculty members asked me for project funding because they know I feel guilty about low salaries."

Fortune-telling. Always dreading the future. Example: "When the president leaves me in charge next week, everyone will slack off."

Black-and-white thinking. Switching from one extreme to another. Example: "If you challenge my appointment of Mary to head the assessment committee, you think nothing of our friendship."

Taking things personally. Putting every decision of others through a filter. Example: "The faculty senate rejected my proposal to embarrass me in front of the faculty."

Taking the blame. Assuming the fault is yours whenever something goes wrong. Example: "Because students didn't come to hear the guest lecturer, I must not have publicized it well enough."

Emotional reasoning. Mistaking feelings for facts. Example: "I am so passionate about the need for a new academic calendar that I am backing it no matter who objects for whatever reason."

Name-calling. Substituting negative names for analyses. Example: "The new faculty are whiners and the old faculty are deadwood—and (as Dilbert might contend) I am an idiot for hiring all of them."

Scaremongering. Thinking the worst. Example: "If she doesn't get the grant, she will sink into utter despair."

Wishful thinking. Imagining all would be well if only something was different. Example: "If only tuition would generate another $100,000, we could add another computer lab."

As positive and clear-thinking as I believe I am, I confess: if I eliminated all these crooked thinking patterns and habits, I would hardly have a thought left. I always turn to such negative thoughts in a crisis; if only I could get out of such distorted reactions, I wouldn't feel like such a totally neurotic worrywart. (See? There I go again!) But how about you?

I am sure that most of us who are in the administrative trenches, working with students and faculty in intensely personal and professional relationships, fall prey to crooked thinking. Butler and Hope encourage us to get a grip on our perspectives. They suggest that we consider the following practices to promote straight thinking:

1. *Watch for pressurizing words.*
   Imperatives like must, should, and have to can start the cycle of negative feelings that distort thinking.

2. Look for extremist words.

Words like *always, never,* and *nobody* lead to exaggerations and generalizations that simply are not true.

3. Consider alternative perspectives.

Is there another way of seeing things? How would the faculty—or the president or a student—look at this issue and deal with it?

College administrators often (note I do not say always) need to step back from their realities and rethink what they say and do. What crooked thinking do you see on your campus—and in yourself? Does distorted deaning threaten your effectiveness? What solutions would you add to the three above?

3

When Does a Professor Cross the Academic Freedom Line?

Have you been following the academic freedom controversy at the University of Wisconsin–Madison (August 2006)? It is an interesting one, raising many issues about the limits of academic freedom, the responsibility for college course content, and the roles of legislatures and administrators in regulating expression in the college classroom. Bloggers have had a field day with this campus brouhaha, and talk show pundits have fanned the flames for the listening public (with one blogger dubbing this "a shout-fest on Hannity & Colmes"). Opinion movers and shakers in the press, on the blogs, at the state house, and from academe are weighing in on both sides of the debate—So why not a parting shot in *Academic Leader*?

If you have missed all this amidst the lazy, vacation days of summer and your (possible) brief respite from the academic wars, let me first bring you up to date on what happened on campus and then briefly review the issues and major arguments, following them with my own thoughts.

The event

Kevin Barrett, an untenured adjunct at UW–Madison, went on a radio program to talk about his opinions on the causes of 9/11, an event he views as a conspiracy that included the US government. (A recent national poll reported that 36 percent of respondents shared such an opinion.) Barrett said he would share his theories with students in a course he had signed up to teach at the university, titled Islam: Religion and Culture. Following a hailstorm of complaints, mostly from the right, the provost, Patrick Farrell, reviewed Barrett's syllabus and reading list. Farrell then issued a statement defending the instructor's right to teach this course at the university: "We cannot allow political pressure from critics of unpopular ideas to inhibit the free exchange of ideas." State Representative Steve Nass declared: "They have academic freedom, but the taxpayers and the legislature have the power of the purse string." And so the battle lines were drawn.

The issues

Implicit in the controversy before and after the provost issued his statement are a number of underlying assumptions that raise important questions. Here are a few of the opinions, in abbreviated form, that are being articulated:

This is a matter of academic freedom, pure and simple. Unfortunately, there is nothing pure and simple about academic freedom. Academic freedom, by tradition derived from the First Amendment to the US Constitution, is not explicitly guaranteed by the Constitution as a fundamental, unrestricted right. In practice, there is a sliding scale of sorts: college professors are accorded the most protection in the educational hierarchy because they teach the most mature students compared to elementary and secondary school teachers. Further, professors are on the cutting edge of developing new knowledge, which suggests a need for greater freedom to explore innovative research and controversial issues with students. Still, as one Supreme Court justice declared, freedom of speech does not extend to yelling "fire!" in a crowded theatre. Has Barrett crossed the line of what is acceptable in the academy?

Barrett crossed the line of what is acceptable in the academy. Ah, well, maybe. Where is that line drawn and who draws it? Some defenders of Barrett suggest that no line can or should be drawn by anyone. He has appropriate academic credentials, having earned his PhD from the UW–Madison, has a syllabus and reading list approved by the provost, and has assured the provost that "students will be free—and encouraged—to challenge his viewpoint." Further, the provost warns us of the slippery slope of censorship: "Silencing that exchange now would only open the door to more onerous and sweeping restrictions." Professors are expected to be responsible in advancing theories, to distinguish between biased personal opinion and merely controversial theories substantiated by research and scholarship. The 1940 American Association of University Professors statement on academic freedom warns that "teachers are entitled to academic freedom in the classroom in discussing their subject, but they should be careful not to introduce into their teaching controversial matter which has no relation to the subject." Does this 9/11 conspiracy theory qualify as relevant and responsible scholarship?

This 9/11 conspiracy theory is not relevant and responsible scholarship. So, some critics contend, Barret is merely taking his impressionable undergraduates into his private prejudices against the Bush administration and high-ranking federal officials. If he can advance such unsubstantiated, crackpot ideas under the guise of academic freedom and intellectual theorizing, then so should these who hold to creation science, intelligent design, or (even) flat earth theories. The course syllabus traces Islam up to 1940. Is it even germane to address 9/11 in this earlier historical context? Has he developed the fact base or other research foundation that would make such theorizing anything akin to responsible scholarship? Will Barret really expose his students to contrary points of view? If not, should an untenured, part-time teacher, at a public university be allowed to promote his personal political views in the classroom?

No untenured, part-time teacher at a public university should be allowed to promote his personal political views in the classroom. This assertion goes to the heart of the protest one hears from the conservative public, legislators, and talk show pundits. Of course, Barrett invited such calumnies by abandoning the classroom for the public airwaves. The part-time, untenured aspect of the case against Barrett should probably be limited only by more careful review of credentials and more supervision and review of course content by department chairs, deans, provosts, or some combination thereof. If the theories are not balanced by counterpoint theories, if students are not indeed encouraged to challenge his viewpoint, if the content is not presented academically with an appropriate research foundation, and if the 9/11 conspiracy theories are not relevant to the course objectives and timeline, then administrators should take appropriate disciplinary action.

While talk show hosts, bloggers, legislators, and others outside of the academy have every right to express their concern, outrage, or disgust, the primary task of ensuring that academic freedom for professors is preserved but not abused must reside in the institutions we serve. In the final analysis, issues like this one require reasoned professional judgment, both by professors and those who are their "academic leaders."

Freedom of Speech Issues: A Legal Primer for Academic Leaders

Today's college campus is a laboratory for the US Constitution's First Amendment provision declaring that government may not "abridge" a citizen's individual rights with respect to five related freedoms: religion, speech, press, assembly, and petition. Public colleges and universities must honor these rights and protect them, but private institutions are not so obligated—unless they commit to them by way of recruiting materials, mission statements, catalogues, or faculty and student handbooks.

Free speech, however, must be balanced by the institution's concern for civility and respect for human welfare. The search for truth in an open and vibrant democracy requires that controversial issues be discussed on campus—in classrooms, special forums, clubs, and elsewhere—with viewpoints that often result in uncomfortable conflicts among diverse groups of students and faculty with different political agendas, personal values, and religious commitments. But there are limits to acceptable free speech. As US Supreme Court justice Oliver Wendell Holmes said in a 1913 ruling, no one can legally yell "fire!" in a crowded movie theater. Free speech but with restrictions—no easy balance for academic leaders in our time.

The nature of "speech" itself has been controversial and the center of many court cases. The First Amendment's freedom of speech clause has been broadened in the process to mean "expression" in its variable forms, including armbands protesting the Vietnam War (the famous 1969 *Tinker v. Des Moines* case is a leading example, with the Supreme Court declaring that neither students nor teachers "shed their constitutional rights to freedom of speech or expression at the schoolhouse gate"); banners (the 2007 Supreme Court ruling in the *Morse v. Frederick* "Bong Hits 4 Jesus" case); and T-shirt slogans and images (see *Diariano v. Morgan Hill*, the 2014 Ninth Circuit decision in an American flag T-shirt case). Many of these cases from public secondary schools set precedents that may or may not apply to similar events at the college level, where students are older and expectations for open debate are greater. But courts do consider these precedents when making rulings in college cases.

It is no wonder that college and university leaders—especially in public institutions—find themselves perplexed about the proper course of action as they try to develop policies and practices that balance the robust and open search for truth with the need for civility and order. What do they do when dealing with issues raised by such events as student protests, controversial visiting speakers, hate speech, charges of "political correctness," internet insults, sexist and racist taunts, and appeals for "trigger warnings" and "safe spaces"? And those are only a few of the current campus speech issues. Other federal court rulings from civil rights laws—such as the Individuals with Disabilities Education Act, Title IX and Title VII, and Section 504 of the Vocational Rehabilitation Act—can also come into play when language that impugns race, gender, or disability is at issue.

Some recommendations

A few recommendations in this primer may help academic leaders make considered decisions for their institutions:

Become familiar with various federal court rulings that may affect your policies. Consider cases like *Sweezy v. New Hampshire* (professor freedom to teach controversial topics), *Keyishian v. Board of Regents* (protecting faculty in "subversive organizations"), *Healy v. James* (regarding controversial student organizations), *Papish v. Board of Curators of the University of Missouri* (protecting questionable language in an underground campus newspaper), *Widmar v. Vincent* (allowing a student religious group to use campus facilities), and *Doe v. University of Michigan* (hate speech codes). Rulings in these suits can give academic administrators some guidance about what the courts may do in cases on their own campuses.

Consult organizations and individuals for information about college speech issues. Your own legal counsel, of course, is always the first place to start. The First Amendment Center at Vanderbilt University has many experts and publications of value to academic leaders. FindLaw is an excellent website for analyses of cases on all educational issues of interest to college administrators. Another good source is the Foundation for Individual Rights in Education (FIRE), an advocacy organization for free speech on campuses that provides detailed descriptions of policies and practices that have met with court sanctions.

Examine all your publications for policies that establish speech expectations. This is particularly important for private institutions because these expectations may be determinative in a suit against the institution. Brigham Young University survived a lawsuit because it had very clear and consistent statements in its materials, catalogues, and handbooks about its given religious values and expectations for student behavior, including speech limitations. If you declare your institution a "bastion of free and liberal learning," as many private colleges do, you may open yourself to challenges on that claim that you do not want and cannot defend. Vague and overly broad handbook requirements are often struck down by courts. (See, for example, the 1989 case of *Doe v. Michigan*.)

Restrict or punish "offensive" digital messages only when you have proper grounds. Courts usually consider digital speech personal and private unless an institution can demonstrate reasonable justifications for restricting such speech. Those justifications might include student handbook statements that are clear and specific, objections to messages that are "lewd, obscene, or patently offensive" (see the 1986 case of *Bethel v. Fraser*), pornography, messages that are deemed "true threats" (specific and capable of being carried out), or claims that are potentially libelous. The 1969 *Tinker* decision also noted that speech that causes a "material and substantial disruption" can also be punished. In our contemporary world, college students are increasingly instant-messaging careless speech over smartphones and other private devices—opening themselves up to legal trouble. Academic leaders can educate them to these potential dangers.

A college or university, whether public or private, provides students a rewarding learning experience and should be, as the Supreme Court put it, "a marketplace of ideas" and a "place of unfettered, robust discussion." Democracy demands and deserves no less. In the 1957 *Sweezy* case, the Supreme Court said: "Teachers and students must always remain free to inquire, to study, and to evaluate, to gain new maturity and understanding; otherwise our civilization will stagnate and die." Knowing the legal parameters of campus speech challenges is a good first step toward successfully achieving and maintaining balance between freedom and order in these controversial times.

Surviving Your Regional Accreditation

M any academic leaders are involved in regional accreditations, and I am no exception. The six regional accrediting agencies are becoming increasingly stringent in the application and interpretation of their standards, and this can make the accrediting process a difficult one to survive. Our institution was a founding member of the Southern Association of Colleges and Schools (SACS) and has been continuously accredited from the beginning. I have been involved in four of the 10-year "reaffirmation" activities, serving as chair of the college steering committee twice and serving as our institutional liaison with SACS for many years.

While I will use SACS as my prototype for a survival guide for fellow academic leaders, I am confident that the strategies I suggest below are equally applicable to any regional—or even specialized—accreditation effort. These experiences are incredibly time-consuming, are increasingly focused on data and student learning outcomes, and can lead institutional leaders to sometimes justified states of paranoia. Nevertheless, you can survive your regional accreditation. Doing so may require you to tap your human resources—diplomacy, organizational skills, patience, and sense of humor—to mention but a few.

Below are five survival strategies I have employed as we have labored through my fourth regional accreditation:

Work on your SACS appeal. This strategy requires you to be attentive to allurements. Of course, when the visiting committee arrives on campus, you want to be sure that your buildings and grounds are in their very best shape. It will not hurt to do whatever you can to encourage faculty and students to manifest their best manners and to show extreme courtesy to the honored visitors. But your SACS appeal can also be enhanced by how you present your documents to the accrediting agency even before anyone arrives on campus. Do you have an attractive cover design? Has your formatting followed all the specified requirements? Do your various documents show your institution in its best light? If not, you may end up making an appeal to SACS to show how you have remedied your weaknesses.

Develop your SACS education program. You should not be surprised to find that many faculty and students are oblivious to the existence of accreditation agencies and have very little idea about their importance to your survival. Both during the self-study process and the follow-up visitation from a committee of your peers, it is crucial that you educate the entire campus to the significance of the enterprise and the nature of its importance to your own survival. Your educational strategies should cover the gamut of your communication processes: regular and special meetings of faculty, students, and trustees; updates and announcements on your campus website; and educational forums to discuss issues and ideas related to the accreditation. Some institutions distribute pencils, mouse pads, coffee mugs, or T-shirts with "core values" or Quality Enhancement Plan (QEP) logos to increase both awareness and enthusiasm for the enterprise at hand.

Practice safe SACS. Often the greatest challenge for academic leaders involved in the accrediting process is the unknown. Will the chair of the visiting committee be reasonable and supportive? Has the steering committee addressed all the standards completely and accurately? Have there been any unanticipated changes in the accrediting agencies operating procedures—or even the development of new standards not yet contained in the accreditor's manuals? You will want to do everything possible to eliminate unanticipated surprises that have a resulted, in part, because you have not protected the institution to the maximum extent possible. This prophylactic function should not be underestimated.

Anticipate SACS harassment. Regional accreditations used to be more social, congenial, and enjoyable than they have become. While you can be reasonably confident that your peers will be well motivated and will understand your responses to standards from your perspective, that may not always be the case. This is, to be sure, a quid pro quo relationship with an outside agency that is responsible for a thorough evaluation: if you give them what they demand, they will give you your desired accreditation. Because regional accrediting agencies have attempted to forestall federal takeovers of the accrediting process—an actual proposal afloat in Washington—they have become determined to be rigorous stewards of institutional quality. For you, this may create the appearance of a hostile work environment as evaluators press you for your information, your cooperation, and your compliance. While you may feel harassed, it is wise to assume the best intentions from those who have "invaded your personal space." They are, after all, just trying to do their job well.

Pursue SACS therapy. At some point, the process will come to an end. Not really an end, you might note, as accrediting agencies will do their best to keep you in line and continually focused on the demands of the agency. This may take the form of probationary status, monitoring reports, or periodic reviews. But once the intensity of the self-study and the visit have been completed, you should take steps to return the campus to its previous state of healthy equilibrium. Celebrate whatever successes you can identify; assure those who have felt wounded that you appreciate their efforts and understand their frustrations. Identify small ways you can reward those who have participated in the process. It is important to develop healthy SACS relations while also helping those on your campus to conclude that the accrediting process is ultimately a very satisfying one—when you have survived. The stress of an accrediting visit can have negative effects, but strong institutions work to address whatever traumas have resulted.

It is unlikely that many faculty or administrators have chosen their professions based on the opportunities they see to enjoy the process of accreditation. Nevertheless, the regional accreditation of your institution is an important mark of success and an essential ingredient in the development of the institution. The survival strategies above are intended to help you think through the best ways to succeed in the face of increasingly complex and demanding accrediting policies and practices. The ultimate objective, however, should not be just to survive such processes but, indeed, to thrive as you help your institution become the best it can be.

Thoughts on the Amenities Arms Race

College amenities have long been a topic of concern for college adminis-trators as well as students and parents. What should college and univer-sity administrators know about such concerns as they examine policies and practices in their own institutions? Here are a few questions for academic leaders and some thoughts about possible answers.

Are more elegant amenities the best way to attract today's new college students?

For those of us who were in college in the good old days of the 1960s, today's emphasis on amenities—such as student activity centers, luxurious meeting spaces for students, several dining room options, climbing walls, fitness centers, and dorm rooms with big-screen televisions—may seem more country club than college campus. But such amenities have been rapidly built since the turn of the new century and sold to college boards and administrators as the best way to attract students who seem more interested in luxury than in learning.

Indeed, research tells us that colleges known for academic excellence are less likely to spend on amenities than on educational quality. For less selective colleges it is easier to construct new buildings than to improve academics, which takes longer and is less visible to parents and applicants. Some critics even accuse college presidents of having an "edifice complex." Expanded athletic facilities may be a case in point. A 2015 study at the University of Michigan found that "lower-tier colleges have a greater incentive to focus on consumption amenities" because their applicants may care more about the "resort experience" and athletic facilities than academics.

But should attracting more students take precedence over improving academic quality?

That is an important question with no easy answer. Perhaps the obvious response is simply why choose? Colleges should do those things that both attract students (including amenities) and enhance their learning strategies and intellectual skills. Those who are on the academic side of the campus dynamic can make sure they advocate for faculty salaries that will attract the best available candidates while doing all in their power to strengthen the curriculum so that students develop critical thinking abilities and academic knowledge of the highest quality possible.

They can also do a better job of connecting and selling academics and career preparation to prospective students. Those on the student life side of the dynamic will no doubt continue to argue for the best possible amenities, athletics, and student services, as they should. Both sides will demand that presidents and boards take their needs and arguments seriously as they compete and cooperate in building effective college policies and practices. This is college politics 101!

What does the future look like for most institutions?

It appears that colleges are entering a new era in which declining student enrollments and rising costs are colliding—with implications for both students and colleges. It is well known that college tuition is rising twice as fast as the cost of living (7 percent versus 3.2 percent), with student debt now exceeding all credit card debt in the nation. Much of that tuition increase seems to result from administrative bloat (ouch!). And the challenge of student debt and college cost—at least some of which is created by the amenities race—is one reason college student enrollment numbers have been stagnant and even declining.

This situation has given rise to the surge in enrollments in less expensive and less luxurious two-year community colleges and the advent of even more online institutions: the University of Phoenix, one such online behemoth, enrolls more students than any other institution in the country. Prestige institutions—think the Ivy League—will continue to thrive in the years ahead, but state institutions and small liberal arts colleges in particular will face ongoing enrollment challenges that require innovative thinking about both student services and academic programs. In a 2015 *Odyssey* article, Aiden Kocarek suggested, surely facetiously, the "5 Things Every College Campus Needs": (1) moving walkways, (2) heated pavement, (3) massage chairs, (4) Starbucks vending machines, and (5) phone charging stations. That may be over the top on the amenities front (although phone charging stations may be a fine idea), but those of us from the 1960s college experience never dreamed there would be climbing walls or private bathrooms in residence halls!

These three questions are central to how colleges and universities will debate directions in the challenging future. I am retired now from one of those fine small liberal arts colleges in the crosshairs of this conundrum, but be assured that I will continue to watch this dynamic play out as my colleagues look for the very best balance between great student services (including amenities) and a challenging academic program.

The Dean's Dirty Dozen

If you have been following my writing for any length of time, you will know that I generally reflect on positive practices and principles that, in my humble opinion, might help deans be more effective in their day-to-day work. I have great empathy with (and sympathy for) deans who work hard to make their colleges better places for all. While I occasionally touch on the downside of deaning—even reflecting on useful Machiavellian principles and insights from Dilbert—I like to stay on the upside of a dean's role and work. For the most part we work with well-educated, highly motivated, and well-intentioned individuals, both in our student population and among our academic colleagues and constituents. But we sometimes encounter the bad apples of the academic orchard.

I do not know how it is on your campus, but below is my personal list of bad apples who more often than not give me academic indigestion.

A dirty dozen

1. *Blame shifters*

   Because we are problem solvers, we often look for the source of our concern. Blame shifters are those individuals in your organization who are never themselves at fault but are quick to tell you who should take the heat. You will never hear a blame shifter say, "I am sorry, I made a mistake, that was my fault, how can I make this right?" A blame shifter's hands are always clean, and such characters make protecting their innocence their number one priority.

2. *Change resisters*

   Some faculty or administrators will spend an inordinate amount of energy not changing, defending the status quo, and holding on to the tried and true. Some change resisters are active in their defense of what is, while others master the fine art of passive resistance. The latter is more frustrating and difficult for deans to deal with. Passive resisters smile and nod and then go back to doing whatever it is they have always done. Active resisters are direct, at least, but are often loud and shrill in their insistence that life must go on just as it has for years and years.

3. *Procrastinators*

Your leadership skills are often sorely tested by those who simply cannot meet a deadline, no matter how reasonable nor how many times you remind them of it. Procrastinators are good at rationalizing and promising—but they can be counted on not to be counted on when a report is due, a schedule is needed, a task must be completed.

4. *Slackers*

While procrastinators usually get their commitments met eventually, slackers have found ways to avoid their responsibilities altogether. Some conveniently forget a meeting, an obligation, or a duty; some declare they are too busy or too unskilled to take on a task; and some spend hours convincing others to take on the job as they themselves weasel out of work that is rightly theirs.

5. *Revenge seekers*

Have you ever noticed that certain faculty or staff never forget a slight (real or perceived) and never forgive an offense? Such individuals seem to collect thorns and devote much of their energy to redirecting them to the most deserving targets. Sometimes, of course, that target is you. Revenge seekers have some misguided sense of justice that requires them to even the score no matter the time or effort required. In fact, getting even is their modus operandi and their modus vivendi.

6. *Manipulators*

I never cease to marvel at skilled colleagues who work in devious ways to arrange life's contingencies so that they end up on top of the heap. Manipulators are often subtle in their usually underhanded efforts to push buttons and pull strings. Such people are adept at playing on emotions and using mind games to accomplish their personal objectives in the give-and-take of academic discourse.

7. *Self-aggrandizers*

There is nothing subtle about some ambitious types who get to the top of the heap by climbing over everyone along the way. They know the tricks of looking out for number one. Self-aggrandizers look over your shoulder at a cocktail party to see whether someone more important might be just around the corner; they are quick to grab the limelight and have inflated their resumes to match their egos.

8. *Whiners*

Because the dean's office is often seen as the complaint department, that office tends to attract a certain group of individuals who want to lodge a concern, and another one, and another one. You see a range of personality types here, some belligerent and obstreperous and some meek and passive. But whiners always have a problem that they think you should fix.

9. *Double dealers*

You doubtless know your double dealers: they know how to play both ends against the middle, but butter wouldn't melt in their mouths. Double dealers will tell you one thing and your provost another; they will play politics for all its worth; they always have a finger in the wind to see which way the academic breeze is blowing today.

10. *Small thinkers*

Small thinkers sometimes have great minds. It is amazing, some-times, to see how petty and insecure adults can be. It has been said that "people with great minds discuss ideas; people with average minds discuss events; and people with small minds discuss people." Small thinkers major in minors and let their priorities be shaped by the insignificant and the unimportant.

11. *Gossip mongers*

Do you know people who thrive on gossip—the more salacious the better? Such individuals in the academic world may even use the classroom to secure tidbits about other faculty members, students, or administrators. Their greatest joy in life is letting you (or some-one else) share in their newfound knowledge about the unfortunate private life of one of your friends or colleagues. Gossip makes their world go around.

12. *Malcontents*

There are some individuals in every college who make their life's work an explicit adventure in making trouble—often for you. Mal-contents seem to have an agenda for action that will create a good deal of risk and excitement for themselves and for everyone they encounter. Somehow, being at the center of controversy and crisis makes their lives worthwhile. It may make yours a living hell.

The good news

Is there good news here? Perhaps so. Examples of such miscreants may be so few and far between that they hardly register on your radar screen. You may actually enjoy the challenge of dealing with such a rogue's gallery of academic individuals—from students to faculty to administrators to your board of trustees—and figuring out strategies that deal effectively with each and every challenge. In fact, you may consider dealing effectively with such people a part of your ongoing on-the-job education as an academic leader. At the very least, you should derive some sense of satisfaction from knowing that the problem people you must deal with where you are may be found elsewhere as well.

So, what's a dean to do?

I have probably not exhausted the list of problem people in a dean's life (surely, you can think of others to send my way), but this short list will serve. Here are a few suggestions for how to keep your spirits up when one or more such characters complicate your academic life:

- Remember that the high-quality clientele on your campus has far more good apples than bad.
- Remember that you expand your human relation skills and administrative talents in the crucible of adversity.
- Remember that you were hired to be a problem solver and that as a middle manager, you are in the people management business.
- Remember that deans on other campuses probably have it worse than you do.

I will bet you have heard it said by some faculty member that your college would be a great place to teach—if there just were no students to put up with. Some deans look at their work with a similar complaint about problem people. Most of us know that our challenge is to stay positive in spite of the occasional work we must do to deal with an imperfect human condition. Deans often work in isolation, with weak or nonexistent support systems. It helps to network with other deans, to keep focusing on the positive, to stay clear of dirty dozen behavior yourself, and to have healthy outlets for frustration that the dirty dozen can create in the workplace. Finally, remember that if we didn't have such problems, we probably wouldn't need deans at all.

The Accountability Conundrum

We hear a great deal these days about accountability in the academy, although few consider this at all mysterious. Many states (including South Carolina, where I try my best to be a "responsible" college administrator) have some kind state law mandating that public schools—and, in some cases, colleges—demonstrate that they are indeed accountable. Typically, this means that institutions file reports that show the institution to be in compliance with certain standards as demonstrated by statistical assessments. (Remember that the art of statistics is the ability to draw a perfectly straight line from a faulty assumption to a fallacious conclusion.) Who could be opposed to *accountability*, a term as revered as *mom* and *apple pie*? The conundrum is in the details: Who is accountable to whom for what?

It might be helpful for academic leaders to reflect on such questions. It seems to me that the concept of educational accountability has morphed through several murky, even mysterious, stages, in less than a straight line from assumptions to conclusions.

Stage 1—The parent is accountable

One of the earliest educational laws in colonial America was a statute in 1642 in Massachusetts, declaring that "the great neglect of parents . . . in training up their children in learning" could result in the court assessing fines to said parents. Churches also took on a major role in ensuring that students were accountable for certain values in the young. Only after the development of schools in the 18th century did accountability for student learning shift elsewhere.

Stage 2—The student is accountable

Once students became the charges of public schools, the expectation was that they would follow the established curriculum, standards of behavior, and evaluation processes. Parents would get report cards showing progress, and if a student was punished in school, the parents would follow suit at home. Such accountability concepts assumed that teachers, administrators, and school board members would make the rules and issue the judgments.

Stage 3—The teacher is accountable

By the middle of the 20th century, testing of students was joined by testing of teachers. Certification of teachers by states often mandated successful passing scores on such standardized tests as the National Teacher's Exam (now itself morphed into the PRAXIS exams developed by the Educational Testing Service). By this time, state departments of education, other governmental agencies, and accrediting bodies were requiring teachers to be accountable for their professional and academic knowledge and performance. State dismissal laws specified "just cause" for firing "incompetent" or "unfit" teachers.

Stage 4—The institution is accountable

This is our current stage, and it extends from the pre-K level through higher education. Today the entire educational system is being held accountable, not merely for the quality of its faculty, curriculum, and facilities (so-called inputs) but also for student learning, behavior, and success—in the school and beyond. To enforce this latest form of educational accountability, institutions have developed elaborate planning and assessment mechanisms and face increasing levels of inspection to see whether "student learning outcomes" have been achieved. If not, accreditation, funding, and reputation are in jeopardy. And now the federal government is itching to make colleges accountable to it.

So, academic leaders, what is next? I have no idea. Dealing with the responsibilities of institutional accountability for learning outcomes keeps me too busy to speculate on the future of this conundrum for administrators. But the longer I am in the trenches, the more I sympathize with poet Ogden Nash, who once observed: "Change is good—but it has been going on too damn long!"

What future do *you* see for accountability in higher education?

4

Rushaholics and Infomaniacs: Discover Your Inner Snail

A personal malady for so many academic leaders can be classified as infomania and rushaholism. While I am far from a computer guru, I know the great value of such technology and have become addicted to email. I am not sure how many hundred such email messages I get each week, but I have an irresistible desire to check and respond to my messages many times a day. Such a compulsion is, I fear, only one symptom of my personal infomania and rushaholism. And I know I am not alone.

Writer Ed Wynn once observed, "Folks used to be willing to wait patiently for a slow-moving stagecoach, but now they kick like the dickens if they miss one revolution of a revolving door." I know what he means, don't you? High-tech communication devices can make us more productive and efficient but making good decisions can be impaired when quantity squeezes out quality. Multitasking only compounds the manic high-speed pace as we rush to process an increasing volume of information.

Being never out of touch—at work, in our homes, and in our cars—has its downside. Leaders need time to muse, reflect, and daydream, and fortunate is the administrator who can locate hassle-free zones for such opportunities to shake off the effects of infomania.

We need to remember that good leaders take time to do things correctly. The key is to work at the right speed, not the top speed. What can we do to find our "inner snail"? Check your email on a regular schedule only once per day. Avoid sending long email responses and instead master the quick reply ("Got it—thanks," "Will do," "When can we meet?" "Call me"). Establish rules for meetings by requiring cell phones and laptops to be turned off. Schedule more face-to-face meetings. Schedule time for meditation. Take a five-minute mental health break every hour. Find one hobby that slows you down, such as painting or gardening. Practice deep breathing while you shower or bathe. Turn off the TV and read a book. Create watch-free days—one day per week when you leave your watch at home.

In his book *Timelock*, Ralph Keyes says, "Just as we looked for ways to speed up life in earlier epochs, now we must find ways to slow it down." Avoid the speed trap of your administrative life by occasionally stepping on the brakes instead of the academic accelerator. Our productivity and peace of mind depend on it.

The Practicality of a Liberal Arts Education

"There is nothing so practical as a good theory," said John Dewey, one of America's most important philosophers. And I say there is nothing so practical as a sound liberal arts education. Academic leaders are sometimes challenged to defend the value of a liberal arts education in a world that seems more interested in promoting preparation for careers and professions. STEM subjects are important—but not to the exclusion of a broader liberal arts education.

The college curriculum today has expanded far beyond the traditional seven liberal arts, in part to answer every parent's question: "So what can you do with your college degree?" Some parents and students focus too soon and too narrowly on specific job training and specialized occupational skills. Such a view can be myopic and, over time, quite impractical. In fact, a 2014 report by the Association of American Colleges and Universities says that at peak ages (55–60 years), those workers who majored in the humanities or social sciences earn annually about $2,000 more than those who majored in professional career–oriented subjects. Want to do well on the LSAT and in law school? Major in philosophy, history, or English.

What is a liberal arts education? Traditionally, this is a curriculum rich in the arts, humanities, sciences, and social sciences. Robert Hersh, president of Hobart and William Smith Colleges, did a survey in 1996 that indicated that 44 percent of high school students were unfamiliar with the term, and both students and parents overwhelmingly believed the reason for going to college was to prepare for a prosperous career. Almost none saw liberal arts as the best preparation for such a career. If anything, this attitude is more prevalent over 20 years later. But if they want to be prosperous, students should take a closer look at the practical value of a liberal arts education.

The liberal arts are more than bodies of subject matter, such as history, philosophy, literature, mathematics, science, and psychology. They are more than vast quantities of information or technical skills. At their best in the college classroom, they constitute the living legacy of the great thinkers *and* doers in the world's civilizations. In the classrooms of dynamic professors, the liberal arts connect learning to life. Mere notetaking will not do; there must be debate, discussion, and dialogue among students and faculty. Students must learn to defend and communicate their thoughts and beliefs in well-argued oral and written discourse. Every career is enriched by such an education—and smart business recruiters know it.

At the heart of the liberal arts is a view of how one learns. Everett Dean Martin, in a 1926 essay entitled *The Meaning of a Liberal Education*, summed it up this way: "One becomes an educated person by virtue of patient study, quiet meditation, intellectual courage, and a life devoted to the discovery and service of truth." In our current era in which "fake news" has emerged as a serious issue for college students (and others), information literacy—developing critical thinking about digital source material—is yet another imperative that a liberal arts education can address. Measurable outcomes are important, but so is the dynamic process of learning itself. As the saying goes, education is more a journey than a destination.

Because that is yet another goal of liberal education: we should expect a liberal arts graduate on their journey to master a number of academic skills that are very practical indeed: study skills, speaking skills, thinking skills, and writing skills, to mention a few. Graduates should also have developed certain values, including civic duty, personal responsibility, respect for people and their traditions, and intellectual honesty. Are not such skills and values central to success in the world of work?

At Converse College, an institution that has always valued liberal learning and where I served as dean, provost, and senior vice president for 30 years, the Founder's Ideal called for an education that would enable students "to see clearly, decide wisely, and act justly." This is a concise summary of the ideal outcome of the liberal arts in action. With such qualities of mind and character, a person can claim to be liberally educated whether the student, to quote Martin again, "has been trained in philosophy or mechanics."

As a more contemporary educator, Cornell University president Frank Rhodes, put it, "The liberal arts are useful in the most significant way of all, useful for the business of living." One might ask: Just how does a liberal education prepare men and women who are better people and better employees in the modern workforce? Here is my view:

First, by grounding students in their own cultural heritage. Surely a contemporary citizen and employee is well served by a study of the past, of the great works of art and literature, of the philosophical explanations of great thinkers who sought answers to the eternal questions: What is good, true, and valuable? Our era is not the only one to encounter such questions as our students consider what is worth knowing and doing in both our present-day groves of academe and an outside world that is fraught with moral dilemmas. Ancient Greek philosophers like Socrates, Plato, and Aristotle provided surprisingly insightful answers to such queries centuries ago.

Second, by broadening the worldview of each student. Students whose field of vision extends across countries and continents will, in our shrinking world, develop a rationale for decision-making, in life and in work, that will keep change in context. College students today may well find their post-college work now a matter of global import as the digital revolution makes communication across countries remarkably easy. As Thomas Friedman has said, the world is now "flat" with digital pathways that erase border security and make the world our neighborhood.

Third, by promoting intellectual inquiry, an active curiosity about the world, and a lifelong love of learning. A sound liberal arts education prepares students for the unpredictability of the future. Mere job training will not suffice, as today's college graduates can expect to be employed in six or more jobs in their lifetimes. Liberal learning teaches students how to ask the important questions, how to solve problems never before anticipated, and how to work with others for the common good. Such abilities will never be made obsolete by change. And these very abilities are exactly what business recruiters and professional graduate degree administrators say they are looking for in today's college graduates.

What an education in the liberal arts does, ultimately, is prepare people for a vocation. An occupation reveals only what you *do*, what you are busy about. A vocation—a calling—bears the stamp of a person's heart, mind, and soul. The liberal arts are avenues into this inner landscape for the students we prepare for the world beyond the classroom. An undergraduate student needs to develop the knowledge and skills not only to earn a good living but, more importantly, to live a good life. In this respect, a liberal arts education is both the most personal *and* practical preparation for life and work we can offer today's college student.

Rethinking Scholarly Publication for Tenure

Well, here we go again. The *Daily Princetonian* reports on its web news page a story about the Modern Language Association's task force recommendation regarding "ways in which universities should rethink how they 'admit' professors and later decide on their tenure." Rosemary Feal, executive director of the MLA, said, "We wanted data that we could analyze in light of the changes in the scholarly community."

Now, lest you think this is yet another effort to jettison the tenure system from the scholarly community, let me hasten to assure you that is not the object of this MLA report. After all, tenure foes are much more likely to come from outside academe than from within—and the MLA is about as "within" as anyone can get. No, this is an effort, as Feal puts it, to respond to the "major changes in the way scholarship is published."

Because colleges and universities—especially top-tier and research-oriented institutions—are increasingly emphasizing scholarship as a condition for tenure, and because it is increasingly difficult for professors to find traditional journals willing and able to accept narrowly focused research articles (partly a consequence of shrinking library budgets), a broader definition of *publication* is desirable. Princeton itself seems comfortable with its current scholarship requirements (according to Dean of the Faculty David Dobkin) primarily because, as Feal observed, "it can attract the greatest experts in their field"—those who have ready access to scholarly journals for their work.

But what about the lesser lights, those faculty squeezed out of the most prestigious research journals? This problem is what the MLA's efforts might rectify. We will await the full report and subsequent action following the author's presentation of results at the annual meeting of the Association of American Colleges and Universities in New Orleans in late January. In the meantime, a few parting shots seem in order.

First, let us ask whether the premise of the report is valid. Logic suggests that it is. No doubt even those nonelite, nonresearch institutions (including small liberal arts colleges) that populate the higher education landscape in the United States have ratcheted up the scholarly publications criteria for tenure over the last decade. And no doubt library budgets and the rising costs of journals work against the publishing prospects of younger faculty without name recognition in the academy. The squeeze is on!

Second, the alternatives to the prestige print journals—notably, the growing respectability of electronic journals—suggest that the new media should not be discounted as legitimate outlets for publication. Peer review is still essential to protect the integrity of the publication process, but faster, cheaper (if not better) forms of publication are likely to grow in popularity and respectability.

Third, recall that the MLA is addressing an old problem, not a brand-new phenomenon. At least as far back as 1990, when Ernest Boyer, on behalf of the Carnegie Foundation for the Advancement of Teaching, published *Scholarship Reconsidered: Priorities of the Professoriate*, leaders in our field have argued for a broader definition of scholarship itself to reflect the interests and needs of what Boyer termed "a new generation of scholars."

So long as the MLA has reopened this issue, let academic leaders consider not only the means of scholarly publication but also the ends. A rereading of Boyer's classic text would be a good beginning place for this aspect of the "publish or perish" tenure conundrum for college professors today.

Given the glut of newly minted humanities PhDs seeking tenure-track positions and the extensive use of adjuncts by cost-conscious institutions, and given the high rate of tenure-track candidates who achieve tenure (about 90 percent by some estimates), there will not likely be much impetus for institutions, especially the most prestigious, to relax or redefine scholarship requirements. And as for those who would argue for the elimination of tenure altogether? That is an argument for another day.

President-Faculty Relations: A Dean's Dilemma?

The situation: You are an academic dean. Your president is one of the new-breed leaders, a nonacademic administrator whose expertise is in business management, alumni affairs, social life, or development. Further, your faculty is a highly organized cohort of professionals who have the security of a tenure system and the strong leadership of a faculty senate. Now your president, in an effort to establish better communication and rapport with faculty, is meeting with individual faculty members, academic departments, and the faculty senate. Do you see a dilemma in your future?

The scenario above is hardly hypothetical. Increasingly, college presidents come from outside the academy, faculties are highly organized and political, and academic leaders advocate communication and "flat" or horizontal decision-making mechanisms. These evolutions in management theory and practice put the administrative role of the dean, the quintessential middle manager, at peril. At the least, deans need to think about how best to accommodate the increased interaction between faculty and president and to make communication a positive experience for everyone.

The concept of "crisis"

We who spend much of our time in the middle know well the challenge of resolving conflicts. We also recall that the Chinese symbol for *crisis* is a combination of the characters for *danger* and *opportunity*. The desire of both presidents and professors to strengthen relations can constitute dangers and opportunities aplenty. Long gone are the days when a dean might recite the dean's dictum: "My job is to keep the president from *thinking* and the faculty from *talking*." (Or is it the other way around?) To succeed in an era when presidents and professors seek common ground, with or without the involvement of the dean, deans must find ways to minimize dangers and maximize opportunities. Otherwise, they will find life in the middle to be one crisis after another.

In my years as a professor and an administrator, I've had opportunities to assess president-faculty relations and to reflect on the dynamics of such relationships. I have been a professor, an academic dean, and an interim president. I seem to be blessed (cursed?) with an ability to sympathize with conflicting points of view, partly because I understand that where you stand depends on where you sit. Because I have sat in many different seats, I can appreciate almost every point of view. That doesn't make solving crises any easier.

The dean's dilemma

As middle manager, deans have the difficult task of communicating faculty needs to presidents and boards while communicating institutional policies and priorities from the top administrative positions to faculty and staff. Unlike some classic business or military chains of command, colleges have shared decision-making processes, which assign distinct spheres of authority to the board, administration, and faculty. The dean's authority is rarely absolute and is often vaguely defined in college management models and faculty handbooks. In fact, a dean "rules" the faculty only by the consent of the governed and with respect and goodwill earned by fair and faithful leadership. One leads the faculty by helping them achieve their best goals, by bringing them together to solve problems and chart new directions, and by skillful consensus building. Part pastor and part policeman, the dean is lost without human relation skills.

Dilemmas, then, assail deans who fail to listen well, refuse to compromise when good sense and good policy require it, or run roughshod over the sensibilities of individual faculty members. But deans also need to take stands, make decisions, and enforce institutional policies. Presidents can complicate the delicate balances and processes that deans and faculties have worked out over the years to promote a relatively amicable and collegial relationship unique to the academic workplace.

The president's laudable intentions can result in an intensified triangulation that creates conflict and confusion. If, say, the president has "heard" a faculty complaint about another faculty member, does that imply "support" for the complainant? If the president asks the dean to "address" the concern, does that require the dean to support the complainant? Are presidents more likely to micromanage the faculty and faculty to lobby the president for pet projects?

Solutions

So, what's a dean to do? While I have no simple solutions to offer, I do think deans can mitigate middle management crises emanating from this triangulation of president, faculty, and dean. Indeed, with some thought, imagination, and planning, a skillful dean can harness the synergy of triangulation and turn what looks like a crisis into an opportunity. When a president wants to establish communication or collaboration or connection with the faculty, a dean might follow with one or more of these approaches:

Reevaluate your relationship with the president. First, be sure that you enjoy the confidence of the president and that your effectiveness with the faculty is not at issue. Next, make sure you and the president have discussed all the dynamics of triangulation and the ground rules you will follow to avoid end runs, divide-and-conquer strategies or other unintended consequences of president-faculty relations. Finally, be sure that you and the president have a common understanding of the goals of such communications and the methods of follow-up.

Reinvent your role as dean. A dean's authority often is more personal than positional (and vaguely defined). Perhaps you need to work more closely with faculty senate leaders—or more effectively with your president to identify academic needs, issues, and priorities. Perhaps you should arrange more conferences for the president *and* you with key faculty in each academic department. A dean's authority is limited, but their autonomy is immense.

Reestablish your reputation for open communications. Communication is not a zero-sum process. If the president wants more communication with the faculty, that does not mean you should have less. Do you invite open communication by word and deed? Do you get out on campus and into faculty workspaces (including classrooms) with regularity? Do you need to remind yourself that your leadership depends on your availability, your ability to hear and appreciate individual concerns, and your responsiveness? The battle scars of deaning can dull our sensitivities and undermine our communication skills.

Deans and other middle managers can fall victim to the dangers of president-faculty relations or find the opportunities every crisis or dilemma creates to become more versatile, more creative academic leaders. The choice is ours.

Student Evaluations of Professors: Another Look

I am a terrific teacher. How do I know? Easy answer: my student course evaluations of me as an instructor consistently conclude that, on a five-point scale, I get a cumulative score of 4.5 to 4.7 on overall effectiveness in the classroom. I know, you may be asking, why not a 5? Well, I never said I was perfect. The beauty of statistics is never having to say you are certain. With this confession off my chest ("terrific" but not "perfect"), I turn now to some analyses.

In an *Academic Leader* column in 2006, I raised questions in an article titled "Student Evaluations of Instructors: A Good Thing?" Those questions cast doubt on the entire process of students evaluating their instructors. I asked:

1. Are students qualified to judge the quality of a professor's pedagogy and academic expertise?
2. Are students evaluating teacher effectiveness—or something else?
3. Are faculty rights to academic freedom compromised by the pressure to secure favorable student evaluations?
4. Are administrators using student evaluations to manipulate faculty behavior?

My answers to these queries were perhaps, possibly, in some cases, and who knows? I quoted philosopher of science Michael Scriven, who surmised, "All student evaluations are face invalid and [less reliable] than the polygraph in criminal cases." I concluded that, indeed, student evaluations of instructors might not be, in the words of Martha Stewart, "a good thing."

Recent research

This issue in higher education continues to generate debate, with arguments from many sides of the controversy. In a 2014 study titled "An

Evaluation of Course Evaluations," researchers Philip B. Stark and Richard Freishtat concluded that "the common practice of relying on averages of student teaching evaluation scores as the primary measure of teaching effectiveness should be abandoned for substantive and statistical reasons." In this study of the evaluation of instructor surveys at the University of California, Berkeley, Stark and Freishtat point out that they are popular because "the measurement is easy and takes little class or faculty time . . . have an air of objectivity simply by virtue of being numerical . . . and comparing an instructor's average rating to departmental averages is easy." We academic administrators like the convenience of simple numbers that seem to measure complex issues like "teacher effectiveness."

So what's the problem? Now that many, perhaps most, colleges and universities use online evaluations, response rates are not nearly as good as for in-class evaluations. Lower response rates, Stark and Freishtat point out, can skew statistical averages, especially because online surveys are affected by student motivation: those who are most unhappy, even angry, are more likely than are happy, satisfied students to complete the survey. In short, if the response rate is low, the data are not likely to be representative of the whole class.

Stark and Freishtat point to a number of other statistical problems with such rating scales: (1) you should not try to average ordinal categories where the numbers are really only labels, not values; (2) rating scales result in averages for a department, but "the mere fact that one instructor's average rating is above or below the departmental average says little"; (3) it makes no statistical sense to compare scores "across seminars, studios, labs, prerequisites, large lower-division courses, required major courses, etc."; and (4) even the student comment section is suspect as students and faculty have quite varied definitions of terms such as "fair, professional, organized, and respectful," and comparing comments across disciplines is difficult.

This recent study concludes that "measuring learning is hard" and that "some students do not learn much no matter what an instructor does." To infer cause and effect requires a controlled, randomized experiment, and student evaluations across myriad subjects and students are hardly that. The scores from the Berkeley instrument do show high correlations between teaching effectiveness scores and ratings for grade expectation, enjoyment of the course, gender, ethnicity, and the instructor's age. These correlations cannot be considered a good thing. If, for example, a professor has rigorous course requirements and grading standards that lead some students to expect low grades, is it fair for those students to give that professor a low rating on effectiveness? Is this an accurate judgment or mere retaliation?

A second recent study by Lillian MacNell, Adam Driscoll, and Andrea N. Hunt (2015) focused specifically on the question of how male and female faculty members are rated by students in college courses. Here was an unusual controlled experiment of online courses. The 43 students in the online course were divided into four discussion groups of eight to 12 students each, with a female instructor teaching two of the groups and a male instructor the other two. Students never saw their instructors. The female instructor told one of her classes she was male, and the male instructor told one of his classes he was female. The end-of-course student rating scale asked students to evaluate the teaching on 12 traits related to teaching effectiveness and interpersonal skills. The instructor the students thought was male received higher ratings on all the traits related to teaching effectiveness and interpersonal skills than did the instructor students thought was female.

MacNell and her coauthors observed that the "male" instructor received markedly higher ratings on professionalism, fairness, respectfulness, giving praise, enthusiasm, and promptness. Granted, the small sample size undermines any claim of scientific validity, but the experiment itself illustrates how one factor—gender—can affect student perceptions and hence their ratings. In this study, the "female" professor was rated a full point lower on the item "returns work promptly" even though both professors returned work on exactly the same schedule.

Now, I am rethinking my claim to be a terrific teacher. It seems to me that a broader, more holistic view of my teaching effectiveness cannot be captured in a single number or even multiple statistical outcomes of student ratings. It has been said that statistics is the art of drawing a perfectly straight line from a faulty assumption to a fallacious conclusion. When it comes to the tricky business of student ratings of instructors, this seems to be the case. The value of such ratings is limited and should be viewed in a broad context; otherwise, a fallacious conclusion is likely. It is more likely that my self-perceived pedagogical excellence is the product of factors such as these:

1. I am a handsome dude (both terms are relevant).
2. I have a good sense of humor (see number 1).
3. I teach majors and prospective majors only.
4. My undergraduate students are Southern women from middle- and upper-middle-class homes, schooled by parents to be respectful and polite to their elders, especially teachers and authority figures.
5. I have always had an impressive title: department chair, division head, dean, provost, vice president, and (even) president.

6. My courses are all on campus, with enrollments of around 12 to 15 students per course.
7. The students are usually capable, positive, goal-oriented, and glad to be in a selective college for women.
8. I expect students to enjoy my classes and to succeed—and my requirements are quite reasonable (as even the students will admit).

Naturally, this is but a partial list of factors that can affect student perceptions of teacher effectiveness and thus their ratings. These "perception enhancements" no doubt inflate my numerical ratings. I am fortunate indeed! But am I a terrific teacher? My answers to that question are much like the ones I provided in my earlier article: perhaps, possibly, in some cases, and who knows? Student evaluations will give instructors and their deans some insight into the students' perceptions of their experiences in the course, but we should not overgeneralize such results with glib conclusions—including one that says I am effective, let alone terrific.

References

MacNell, L., Driscoll, A., Hunt, A. (2015). What's in a name? Exposing gender bias in student ratings of teaching. *Innovative Higher Education,* 40(4), 291–303.

Stark, P., & Freishtat, R. (2014). An evaluation of course evaluations. *ScienceOpen Research.* Retrieved from https://www.scienceopen.com/document/read?vid=42e6aae5-246b-4900-8015-dc99b467b6e4

Assessmania and Bureaupathology in Higher Education

This is not a rant. As a college administrator, I am fully aware of the importance of assessment and the bureaucratic efficiencies mandated in higher education in our country today. But I do think it is important for academic leaders to be able to step back from the fray and the daily demands of administration and think about the philosophical and educational implications of the standards movement in higher education. Most college and university administrators are keenly aware of the standards movement in K–12 public school education, a dominant theme of contemporary education reform that has now moved to the college campus.

This movement has created a significant amount of controversy, with strong proponents on both sides of the issue. Many argue that it is essential for colleges and universities to embrace the standards movement and to verify their educational value (which now comes at what may seem an extraordinary cost to the public) by way of comprehensive and sophisticated assessment systems. In the public school sector, this is often announced to the public by so-called report cards for schools, required by the sweeping federal legislation known as No Child Left Behind.

In higher education, we are now finding similar reform movements accompanied by increasing demand for quantitative proof (or at least some evidence) to justify the high cost of a college education. Some argue that this has now become the primary responsibility of accrediting agencies—not only regional accrediting bodies but also the myriad of specialty accreditations for an extensive array of professional and disciplinary curricula. This alphabet soup of accrediting agencies includes such formidable bodies as NASAD (art), NASM (music), NLNAC (nursing), NCATE (education),

FIDER (interior design), and AACSB (business), to mention but a few. These agencies have done much in recent years to base accreditation processes and decisions on outcomes rather than inputs. The major concept here is that a college and its programs should be measured not by the qualifications of its faculty, the claims made in catalogs or on syllabi, or the library and other resources in the institution but rather by student performance in both qualitative and quantitative measures of achievement.

For institutions of higher learning, the consequence of this paradigm shift has been the creation of a wide range of assessment procedures—many of them emphasizing the quantitative side of the equation—to provide these agencies with the outcome evidence required to show that the accreditation standards have been met. Some argue that such measures are essential to convince a skeptical public that there is value in the educational commodity for which they are paying a premium. Others point out that the accrediting agencies are serving a purpose that they are uniquely qualified to provide and that may well stem the tide of heavy-handed governmental impositions of accountability.

Questions

These arguments may indeed be true. Nonetheless, it seems to me appropriate for educational leaders to reflect on a number of questions that follow from this now reigning concept of accountability and accreditation:

Are the premises of the accountability movement in higher education justified? This is to say that there may be reason to question the notion that outcomes should replace inputs, that quantitative score keeping is the best way to determine the value of educational services, that the public is truly skeptical of the utility of investment in a college education, and that government is ready to leap into the breach if accrediting agencies do not save the day. This is also to question the premise that standards established by external agencies—which are granted the authority to close or sanction programs or entire institutions—should guide (or even control) the mission, policy, and curriculum of higher education. Are these premises in fact true and compelling?

Are the requirements for assessment—and the vast bureaucratic mechanisms required to generate the data—worth the cost and effort? This question should be considered within the context of any individual institution of higher learning, but there is reason to contend that the scarce resources of an institution might better serve the mission of the institution in some other activity or enterprise. To answer this question, it would be necessary to calculate the cost of personnel, hardware, software, committee structures, report generation, and so on and determine whether the cost justifies the commitment and resources allocated. But as long as accrediting agencies have the power to demand such outcome evidence, institutions may have no alternative. Are there any possible alternatives?

In the long run, does this kind of outcomes-based accountability lead to improvements in educational institutions? Accrediting agencies typically go beyond merely requiring the collection and reporting of data to insist that institutions aggregate, disaggregate, and analyze data and from that process determine specific improvements that should be made to all aspects of the institution's operation. Such processes must be continuous and a part of assessment reports. Are these requirements leading to the most important and desirable improvements in the institution? For example, would more subjective and qualitative measures result in harder-to-validate but better institutions?

Again, this is not a rant but rather a plea for institutions to take opportunities for reflection on the accreditation processes that presumably ensure institutional effectiveness. As ingrained as the standards movement has become, with its concomitant requirement for comprehensive assessment systems to measure outcomes, it would nonetheless be a mistake for academic leaders to merely assume that such processes and activities ensure a better institution. What is the most appropriate relationship between internal and external locus of control when it comes to higher education policy decisions? There are points at which assessment can become a mania and bureaucratic processes become pathological. We may simply go through the motions to produce results that bypass the best thought and evaluation required for truly effective education. Some academic leaders are rightly concerned that the demands of "outcomes accountability" may undermine rather than enhance the intellectual joy and creativity of the college classroom, establishing a tail wagging the dog approach to education that may not be in the best interest of students or faculty. Let us, then, take time to pause and reflect—and then determine platforms and positions that make the most sense for higher education.

5

So, What's a Provost?

I have had a lot of positions in my professional career—from professor to president—but my present title is one that provokes puzzlement, even among some in the academy. Everyone knows (or thinks they know) what a department chair, division head, dean, or vice president is and does. But many a person will give me a quizzical look and ask, "You're the *provost*? So, what's a provost?" My flip response is that a provost is like the superintendent of a cemetery: both have a lot of people under them, but none of those people are listening. A clever response, I tell myself, but not really helpful. Let's think more seriously about what a provost is.

While job descriptions will vary from institution to intuition, the work and role of the provost is quickly becoming a standard administrative post in many colleges and universities. In a 1998 survey by the Council of Independent Colleges (CIC)—an organization made up primarily of smaller institutions—23 percent of chief academic officers (from 381 respondents) indicated that they have the title of provost. This administrative title has typically been reserved for larger institutions, but that is changing quickly. So what is a provost? Let me take a stab at a working definition as well as a rationale for the emergence of such an academic administrator.

Definition

Etymologically, *provost* comes from the Latin for "placed first." The dictionary provides an interesting array of more specific definitions, including these: (1) the chief dignitary of a collegiate or cathedral chapter, (2) the chief magistrate of a Scottish burgh, (3) the keeper of a prison, and (4) (a definition that informs without clarifying) a high-ranking university administrative officer. Actually, I sometimes think definition number 3 comes closer to my work than any other. (Perhaps that is why faculty keep sending me *Dilbert* cartoons!) In most cases, the provost in a college or university is simply the chief academic officer and typically is the administrator in charge when the president is off campus.

As a practical matter, the increasing number of provosts in higher education can be traced to the evolution of management systems within the academy. There are, in my opinion, several forces shaping this evolution, including these:

Colleges have become more bureaucratic. Colleges, even small ones, have become in our time extraordinarily complex organizations. Compliance with government regulations, financial aid formulas, institutional assessment requirements, accreditation reports from a variety of agencies, legal action against the college (35 percent of chief academic officers in the CIC survey said they had been involved in a lawsuit), and formalized tenure and promotion processes—these are but a few of the complexities that have required institutions to rethink administrative structures. Department chairs have not escaped the fallout from this trend. While they often prefer to be viewed as professors, they are being moved by bureaucratic imperative into ever-greater administrative roles. There are, simply, far more management functions in the contemporary college.

The role of the college president has changed. While a high percentage of college presidents continue to come from academic backgrounds, the qualities required for success in the top administrative position increasingly depend upon business, fund-raising, and public relations skills. Few presidents these days are able to perform as academics; they are much more likely to be like corporate leaders. As the president becomes more of the high-visibility, externally focused leader of the institution, the need for an internally focused academic leader becomes imperative. Provosts are seen as those internal leaders charged with oversight of academic programs—but also many other supervisory duties. These might include athletics, student services, and admissions.

Title inflation has changed the management structure in many institutions. Compared to even a decade ago, college catalogues will reflect a growing number of administrative positions. For example, as colleges provide more student services, there will be more directors of academic support centers, directors of counseling, directors of student activities, directors of computer services, and other "mid-management administrators." Clerical staff that used to be limited to "secretaries" will now include "administrative assistants." In like manner, an academic unit may have several deans and associate deans, all of whom now report to a vice president of academic affairs. Someone who could handle virtually all of the major requirements of academic administration 20 years ago might have been simply "the dean," while today that individual holds the more elevated title of "the provost."

A look to the future

In all probability, we will see more and more colleges with provosts. The chief academic officer will likely become the chief operating officer. This is to say, colleges—even small ones—will take on the characteristics of corporations. The administrative demands on institutions, explained in part by the factors above, will mean more administrative work to be done. Colleges are no longer informal, rustic, idyllic institutions where teachers and students live lives characterized by freedom and flexibility. Those days, unfortunately, are long gone. Consequently, department chairs in the future will teach less and manage more—more budgets, reports, studies, and administrative functions. Few faculty in my experience feel called to such responsibilities, and few have the preparation or training of their counterparts in the corporation. Nor does the reward structure address the increasing demands on department chairs to be administrative leaders. That will need to change. Department chairs, deans, and provosts will become the management team for the internal administration of the college while presidents become roving ambassadors and fund-raisers.

That students increasingly go to college to get credentials and certifications for career advancement contributes to the changing nature of the college itself—including the management of academic policy and practice. Department chairs, no less than deans and provosts, will surely see their roles continue to evolve toward a management definition and away from a professorial definition. The growing expectations for customer service and accountability in high education ensure that direction. In the CIC survey only half of chief academic officers indicated that they continue to teach. In some ways the more formalized structures are both useful and necessary—but we are also losing some of the academic energy and intellectual substance at the heart of the college experience. That is likely to be exacerbated by current trend lines for colleges of the future.

Ideally, those who ascend to the office of provost will remember to keep teaching and learning at the center of their self-definitions. If a provost is one placed first, I hope it is not as the keeper of the prison but as the keeper of the light of learning.

Checking Out? You Need an Exit Strategy

"I never think of the future—it comes soon enough."

—Albert Einstein

It has been said that old deans never die; they just lose their faculties. A clever saying, that—and it reminds those of us who have been stomping around the academic vineyards for many years that we ought to have a well-considered plan for when all signs point to our need to hang it up. I have been in higher education for nearly 50 years as a faculty member and administrator and have been thinking that it is time to let the youth movement take over. After all, any college or university that expects to survive in these challenging times will need fresh ideas and dynamic new leadership to keep the academic ship afloat. With MOOCs, demands for online academic options, high-tech innovations, accreditation interventions, government regulation at all levels, and ever-greater customer service expectations from students and their helicopter parents, a new generation of academic leaders must be cultivated and counted on to show the way.

So, if you think it may time for you to go, what is your exit strategy? And if you are not sure it is time to go, how might you discern the clues and (sometime subtle) signs that a graceful exit might be in order? Let me try to answer these two questions, starting with the second.

Looking for clues

How do you know it is time to hang it up? Here is a David Letterman–style top ten clues list to consider:

10. After lunch, you feel a nap coming on.

9. On a nice spring day, you wonder whether the golf course is open yet.

8. Your secretary or administrative assistant is out sick, and you start to panic.

7. You have no new email messages in the morning—and you are delighted.
6. When the stock market news is good, you refigure your 403(b) retirement account totals.
5. You forget an important committee meeting.
4. When you ask what went on in that meeting, your colleagues did not notice you missed it.
3. You are invited to more retirement events but fewer faculty parties.
2. When you open the morning paper, you go first to the weather, then to the obituaries.
1. Your boss does not seek your wise counsel on decisions that affect your work.

There may be other signs, of course—like when your administrative colleagues begin to admire the fine office space you currently occupy—and you sense that they can imagine themselves sitting at your desk. But no need to get paranoid! Enjoy the compliment and remember that this fine office is only yours on loan from your institution.

Exit strategies

Once you have decided that the time has come to transition to a kinder, gentler lifestyle, you will want to plan an approach to this change that suits you and your institution. In preparation, you should no doubt do some reading on retirement options—such as Clay Schoenfeld's classic *Retirement 901: A Comprehensive Seminar for Senior Faculty and Staff* and the many good advice articles in the AARP magazine and bulletin you have been perusing for years—and have some serious discussions with your family and your financial advisers. Making sure your health care provisions are adequate is just one more essential aspect of an exit plan, ever more complex as the Affordable Health Care Act unfolds in stages. Such decisions should receive plenty of deliberations and collaborative discussions as a prelude to leaving the scene. Schoenfeld advises senior faculty and administrators to be sure, before heading off into retirement, to ensure they have the "Triple A Essentials": adequate income stream, affordable health care, and activities for self-fulfillment—good advice for all of us old timers.

Some of us nearing the end of (one hopes) fulfilling careers as faculty or administrators or both might find one of the following exit plans just right for us, remembering that no one size fits all.

Cold turkey. Depending on one's plans, predilections, and preferences, it may be best to cut the tie that binds and walk away. As the saying goes, however, you should not retire from something but to something. Those with second career options may want to make a clean break with their college or university and plunge full-time or part-time into new work that is satisfying and rewarding, personally and financially. Many who are drawn to the academic life—as teachers or administrators—have strong service interests. A cold turkey retirement can provide time to engage more fully in one's community needs or service opportunities in the wider world beyond. Some faculty or academic deans may have books unwritten that now become "shovel-ready" projects; others may find consulting, joining search firms, or turning some avocation into a business the ideal exit plan. But do retire to something.

Phased retirement. In recent years, the concept of phased retirement has become an increasingly popular option for those faculty and administrators who want to transition more slowly into the retired life of seniors. My college has adopted such a program, and I have just started the first of three years of half-time employment with a college I love and have served for 42 years as a faculty member, department chair, division head, dean, vice president for academic affairs, provost, interim president, and (now) senior vice president. I still am able to teach three courses and serve on 10 committees while working with assessment and accreditation initiatives as an administrator. And if I want to I can go home after lunch for a nap and a good walk around my neighborhood before my evening, heart-healthy glass or two of red wine. Lacking many hobbies or avocations, this is an ideal exit plan for me—and maybe for you.

Part-time teaching. A third option that may work well for some academic leaders is a variation on a formal phased retirement plan (which may not even be available in many institutions): part-time teaching. Many if not most deans and provosts started their academic careers in the classroom. The opportunity to return full circle could be an ideal way to ease into the next phase of life. This might rekindle academic interests that have been crowded out by the constant demands of the administrative work that has grown ever-more burdensome and less rewarding over the years. It might be an opportunity to take on some interesting research too, investigations that might lead to more stimulating pedagogical techniques, technological skills, or content knowledge that can make teaching exciting and new. This option can leave plenty of time for travel, taking or auditing courses at one's own institution or elsewhere, and reading those books that have been on the bucket list for years.

The long (or short) goodbye. As the old popular song put it, "Breaking up is hard to do." Whether one has been at an institution for a long time or for a brief sojourn, leaving can be difficult. Many retirees from academe lament that they do not miss the work, but they do indeed miss the people. And some even miss the work. In any event, life does go on. Yogi Berra supposedly said life changes so fast that "even the future isn't what it used to be." Kehlog Albran, in *The Profit*, observed: "I have seen the future and it is very much like the present—only longer." Antonio, a Shakespeare character in *The Tempest*, declares that "what's past is prologue." All these speculations about the future may be—in some sense or other—accurate for those of us contemplating the culmination of our academic careers. Will your post-career future be radically different from the present? A continuation? A variation built on the experiences of the past?

I do hope Shakespeare's King Lear was wrong when he said, "'Tis our fast intent to shake all cares and business from our age, conferring them on younger strengths while we, unburdened, crawl toward death." I have no intent to crawl anywhere and hope that may be true for any academic leader who is looking at saying goodbye to old friends. Our experience and wisdom may yet serve those who rise to take our places as we mentor future academic leaders, sharing with them both the burdens of office and the many joys of teaching and administration. Our academic experience can still be useful to the next generation of professors and administrators. As Søren Kierkegaard tells us, "Life can only be understood backwards, but it must be lived forwards." Our understanding, gained from success and failure, can help those who take our places enjoy successful careers "lived forwards" in the academy.

By the year 2030 the entire baby boom generation will be senior citizens, well into the retirement lives of their choice. Those who have chosen the academic life will have made their mark on the lives of countless college students and colleagues along the way. May all of them, and we who precede them, find the best path into happy and fulfilling new lives after our work lives are over, checking out with well-planned exit strategies and miles to go before we sleep. And may you retiring deans keep all your faculties.

My Last Commencement Speech

"The world will little note nor long remember what we say here."
—Abraham Lincoln

In 1863 Abraham Lincoln punctuated his famous Gettysburg Address with one of the most inaccurate predictions in American history. As Senator Charles Sumner later observed, "The world noted at once what he said and will never cease to remember it. The battle itself was less important than the speech." That is what I would like to be said about my last commencement speech. While I have sat through more than a hundred commencements as a dean and provost and given several commencement speeches to schools and colleges over my long career, it would be hubris indeed to suggest that much of what I said was remembered by anyone.

As I was listening to my car radio on a recent road trip, an NPR reporter was interviewing a long-time college president and asked this intriguing question about the many commencement speeches he had heard: "Other than 'reach for the stars' and 'work hard to achieve your dreams,' have you ever heard a commencement address that expressed some unusual unforgettable theme?" That got me thinking about what kind of commencement speech I might possibly invent that had even a ghost of a chance of being remembered by graduates who have many other things on their mind—like not tripping when they walk across the stage to get their diploma—than trying to remember what a commencement speaker has said.

I suppose I could try to say something humorous, but humorist Dave Barry beat me to that with his commencement address to a college class in 2006. Here is what he said on that occasion:

> This is your big day—the day when you jam four years' worth of un-laundered underwear into a Hefty bag and leave college, prepared by your professors to go out into the Real World. The first thing you'll

notice is that your professors did not go out there with you. They're not stupid; that's why they're professors. They've figured out that college is a carefree place where the most serious real problem is finding a legal parking space. So, your professors are going to stay in college until they die. Even then, they'll go right on teaching classes. This is called "tenure."

You have to admit, that's very clever and perhaps more accurate than we college administrators would like to think. I think that I might as well stay with the tried and true, so here it is in a nutshell my last commencement speech:

Students, I congratulate you on reaching this milestone in your education. I know you are in a hurry to get your diploma, so "the world will little note nor long remember what we say here." Would that I be half as wrong as Abraham Lincoln was when talking about his unforgettable Gettysburg Address. But on the hope that you might hold on to two ideas that seem to be the staple of most commencement addresses, let me urge you to keep these two imperatives in mind:

Reach for the stars. Yes, stars are beyond our grasp, but as poet Robert Browning said, "A man's reach must exceed his grasp or what's a Heaven for?" Surely, today we would also say that women should reach for the stars too. Set your goals high, and always think of yourself as a highflyer.

What "stars" can you reach for? For some of you that might be a graduate degree, perhaps the next step in an education you have only just begun. (Remember that the word *commencement* means to "commence" or "begin," not to "end.") What you have accomplished in your first four years of college is a launching pad for something greater beyond these hallowed halls. As you know, a graduate degree pays off in higher income over the course of your lifetime, but beyond that benefit a graduate degree will enhance your knowledge and skills in ways that will strengthen your personal and professional abilities.

For others, the stars might be defined by the world of work, a vocation where you can immediately begin applying your skills, not just those practical and technical skills you acquired in courses and internships but your creative and intellectual skills as well. Employers want new hires who can add value to their organizations, blending into their workforce as enthusiastic, cooperative, eager-to-learn workers with potential for productivity and growth. Will you be a "stellar" (a word that means "star power") employee?

Still others of you new graduates may seek adventure in service and travel, perhaps in the Peace Corps or AmeriCorps. For you the future is bright as you become shining examples of people who fulfill themselves and their destinies in helping others in that big world beyond the horizons of this time and place.

Whatever you do and wherever you go, remember that you take the education you received here with you. As you figure out what life holds for you—and you for it—aim high. Your reach should indeed exceed your grasp. We hope you will *become* a star. As you contemplate that destiny, reflect on these wise sayings:

- "Not all dreamers are winners, but all winners are dreamers. Your dream is the key to your future. The Bible says that 'without a vision (dream), a people perish.' You need a dream, if you're going to succeed in anything you do."—Mark Gorman
- "Far away there in the sunshine are my highest aspirations. I may not reach them, but I can look and see their beauty, believe in them, and try to follow where they lead."—Louisa May Alcott
- "Aim higher in case you fall short."—Suzanne Collins

There are things to think about as you contemplate your future. Now, the second imperative:

Work hard to achieve your dreams. Surely you have learned by now that success is not handed to you on a silver platter. As the saying goes, you must plan your work and work your plan. Benjamin Franklin noted, "Those who fail to plan, plan to fail." Be assured that in the world beyond—just as was probably true in college—you will encounter people who outshine you in intelligence, personality, and good looks. Yes: sad but true. But no one need outshine you in effort. Too many students wake up to find their dreams have vanished into the morning mist.

Here are some wise sayings to think about as you plan your work and work your plan:

- "If you have built castles in the air, your work need not be lost; that is where they should be. Now put the foundations under them."—Henry David Thoreau
- "We are designed with a dreaming brain and a hopeful spirit; it is our nature to envision the life of our dreams. And while dreaming comes easy to us, we must never forget that it takes strength, dedication, and courageous action to bring that dream to life." —Steve Maraboli

- "Perseverance is the hard work you do after you get tired of doing the hard work you already did."—Newt Gingrich
- "The reason a lot of people do not recognize opportunity is because it usually goes around wearing overalls looking like hard work." —Thomas Edison
- "Hard work spotlights the character of people: some turn up their sleeves, some turn up their noses, and some don't turn up at all." —Sam Ewing

So, there you have it: two simple imperatives—reach for the stars and work hard to achieve your dreams. Dream it, plan it, do it. Follow that star and follow these directions for *reaching* the stars. As Yogi Berra assures you graduates, "If you don't know where you are going, you'll end up someplace else."

Delightful Deaning

You know, dean colleagues, I sometimes wonder what keeps me in this wacky enterprise of academic administration. After all, ours is not the happiest of professions. Indeed, it is frightfully easy for us to dwell on the downside of deaning. When you drag your weary body home at the end of a typical day in the academic vineyard, what do you tell your spouse or companion or dog? How often do you say, "What delightful deaning I did today"?

My guess is, you are more likely to review the tale of woe that was yours in the vale of tears that is the dean's venue. If my guess is correct, it may be for some predictable reasons.

The downside of deaning

Deans often find themselves in positions that raise their blood pressure and lower their morale. Why so?

They are caught in the middle management morass. This simply means that they get delegated to from above and below—and rarely have the authority to meet the demands and expectations of the delegator.

They are keepers of the complaint department. Every institution needs some office where complaints, disputes, criticisms, dilemmas, exasperations, outrage (have I covered them all?) can be recorded. In colleges that is the dean's office.

They are charged with maintaining order while also initiating change. Maintaining order usually requires reinforcing established rules and values while initiating change requires just the opposite. This can create a Hobson's choice—and lead to allegations that the dean is inconsistent or hypocritical or both.

I could go on, but you get the idea. No wonder the turnover rate for deans is so high: deaning is often a desultory business.

Delightful deaning

To counter the downside of deaning, we need to remember the delights that keep us coming back for more, day after day and year after year. After all, staying positive and upbeat is not only a dean's duty but one of the keys to your success. Consider some of these rewards of your role and work:

Power. Yes, I know, you have far less than you need in the college life when faculty consider themselves your superior, presidents and boards micromanage your every move, and the customer (student) is king. But your office does give you considerable authority to influence policy and effect change. Your power depends on personality, ingenuity, human relations skills, and earned credibility—as well as formal definition— but you have opportunities aplenty to delight in decisions.

Prestige. College deans still are well regarded, both in the academy and in the community. Sure, you have your detractors, but almost all opinion surveys now rank college deans above even physicians in terms of prestige. Few academics rise to our exalted (even revered!) position. Your title signifies recognition based on a combination of academic, administrative, and personal qualities that identify you as a highly qualified professional in a prestigious vocation.

Performance. If you do your work well, you can enjoy the intrinsic rewards of self-satisfaction. You have more freedom than most professionals to set your own goals, to choose interesting and innovative projects, to interact with an extraordinary array of individuals on the campus and in the academic world. You can continue to teach (if you want to); you can travel abroad and attend worthwhile conferences at home; you can write for journals like *Academic Leader*. Few indeed are the professionals who have such performance opportunities.

Professionalism. Speaking of performance opportunities for professionals, you should count among your privileges the opportunity to grow as a professional. The opportunities you have to develop management and leadership skills are almost limitless. In the dean's office, you can stay in touch with other deans through professional organizations, attend seminars and conferences devoted to refining your professional abilities, and read widely in the expanding body of literature (online or in library) addressing administrative issues. We who are in the learning business should rejoice at opportunities to learn more about our own work.

Beyond the four points above, we can find pleasure in almost every other aspect of our work. We get to reward faculty and recognize student honors. We can attend college concerts, plays, art exhibits, and athletic events—and call it work. We work on beautiful campuses (most of us) and with civil, congenial colleagues (most of them). These are joys not to be taken lightly nor for granted. Amidst the pressures and problems of deaning, we can find (and celebrate!) the delightful aspects of deaning. These are the things that keep me in the wacky enterprise of academic administration.

A Dean's Destination

Do you know where you are going? I am not thinking here about all the things deans must do to lead their faculties by way of some systematic strategic planning process, goal-setting workshop, or performance objectives enterprise. No, this month I am thinking about career directions individual deans might pursue as they consider their professional options. As futurist Joel Barker advises, "Don't mistake the edge of your rut for the horizon."

Sometimes the incessant business of the day-to-day academic world leaves deans precious little time to escape from the alligator pit to consider whether fighting the alligators is worth the effort. Do you find time to plan your personal future? Have you thought about what options there are for people with your experience and skills—whether that is inside or outside the academy? Are you a settler or a sojourner? Where would you like to see yourself ten years down the road?

Destinations

Anyone who has the knowledge, skills, and motivation to take on the daunting dilemmas of deaning is likely to be someone who could contemplate a number of successful destinations. Some, like relief pitcher-philosopher Dan Quisenberry, might simply conclude that "I have seen the future, and it is much like the present—only *longer*." Or they might agree with what, in the film, Bonnie said to Clyde: "We thought we wuz goin' somewhere, but we wuz just *goin'*!" The life of a dean is a stressful but also rewarding profession and one worth staying with if you are a settler and find your work continually satisfying and self-renewing. But sojourners might consider other such options as these:

Moving up the academic ladder elsewhere. For the successful dean there are always bigger and better institutions to serve, and it is not unusual to see deans scanning the ads in the *Chronicle of Higher Education* to see if there might be bigger fish to fry. Not to at least contemplate such options is to limit your creative "futurizing." Moving up and out to bigger deanships is a career path many deans choose.

Moving back to the classroom. Some deans, especially those who may be nearing the end of a long deaning career and those who want to stay at their present institutions, ought to consider seriously the prospects of reascending to the professoriate. That is easier in some disciplines than others, of course, but if you have kept your hand in classroom teaching, kept up with your academic discipline, and maintained at least the vestige of a research and writing program, classroom teaching is an honorable end game.

Moving into different academic positions. An attractive option for some deans is to consider openings that provide new administrative challenges. That might mean moving up to a vice-president or provost position, whether in the home institution or elsewhere. Successful administrative experience at the dean's level is the ideal preparation for expanded administrative responsibility. Such positions may even lead eventually to a college presidency. To move in this direction, you have to love the administrative life and the even greater political challenges such positions present.

Moving out of academe. For some deans who want to test their skills outside of academe, there are a host of leadership positions in higher education and the business world. Some deans gravitate to state agencies governing colleges and universities, while others find the opportunities to travel that consulting presents exciting new directions to consider. Any dean who successfully leads a faculty of any size will find leadership opportunities aplenty in the outside world. Some initiate publishing businesses; others find creative outlets for their problem-solving skills in established industries or start-up internet enterprises.

When all is said and done, we must confess that (as the aphorism puts it) "one who lives by the crystal ball learns to eat ground glass." Or to put this another way, as Woody Allen said, "If you want to hear God laugh, tell him your plans." Nevertheless, thinking about alternative futures for yourself is one way to energize your present work wherever you have been plying the fine art of deaning. And if your future is "much like the present—only longer," you might find it helpful to read Clay Schoenfeld's helpful little book entitled *Retirement 901*. A final aphorism, this one by Karen K. Clark, for you to think about: "Life is change. Growth is optional. Choose wisely."

A Dean's Demise

Not long ago, I saw a dean dying. Oh, I do not mean that literally, but rather I could see the dean wilting on the vine. First goes the sparkle in the eyes, then the enthusiasm and optimism in the speech, then the posture and speed of movement; finally, there is grim resignation. Like most deaths, this one was a long time coming and seemed to be the culmination of a process of letting go of the energy and effort it takes to sustain a dean's life. The psychological wear and tear on a dean leads to a shorter life span than is true for many others in the academic world, perhaps excepting college presidents. Last year, another good dean colleague of mine rejoiced in a decision to return to full-time teaching at his same institution as a welcome release from the pressures of deanly duties. This dean's life too came to a premature end—although he lives to tell about it. What factors contribute to a dean's demise?

The lifecycle of a dean

While generalizations can be dangerous, I think most deans go through a discernible lifecycle. Because of their degree of formal education and requisite experience as a faculty member (usually with enough time to rise to at least the associate professor level), deans come to office relatively late in life. Their education and experience have led them to believe that they have leadership abilities that can best be exercised in the office to which they aspire. Some campaign actively and apply widely to achieve this administrative position; others are persuaded by presidents or colleagues to fill a vacant position where few good applicants exist. Either way, the dean comes into office with fresh ideas and joyful anticipation about changes that will make the college a better place for faculty and students. This is stage one of a dean's life cycle, a stage we might call *the quest for office.*

The next stage is a too-short, blissful period during which the dean is congratulated, oriented, introduced to the college and the outside community, and invited to both academic and social occasions galore. At this point the dean's philosophy, recommendations, and plans are sought by everyone from the board chair to the department chair. This glorious stage, stage two, we shall call the *honeymoon*.

Next, the dean enters a period of sustained energy and effort during which a settling-in process ensues. The dean works hard to build constituencies and allegiances while attempting to reverse the poor decisions and weak leadership of the previous dean. The new dean's ideas are loudly applauded, and academic policies and programs undergo a refreshing renewal. This stage is one of great productivity, a stage characterized by innovation and success. Call stage three *the golden years*.

After a few years in stage three, there is often (but not always) a mellowing period in which the dean generates less energy and fewer innovations. The dean may become more interested in service to the academic world beyond the college or may reflect on lost joys of classroom teaching. In this period, they will have made both mistakes and enemies, and a new generation of faculty and students will have forgotten the golden years. Some deans become cynical, some move on to new institutions, some hunker down to deal with a never-ending series of conflicts and crises. The bloom is off the rose. Call stage four *the survival stage*.

Finally, the dean wears out, becomes jaded, and gives up the ghost. Energy has been replaced by lethargy and idealism has given way to cynicism. The dean is no longer in touch with the life force of the institution—the vital and sustaining ideas that drive the academic enterprise. Let's call stage five *the demise*.

Staying alive

This lifecycle above may not be true for you, but it is for many deans. The amount of time it takes to go from stage one to stage five may be quite short or very long. In spite of the opening aphorism, all deans die. The challenge is to withstand the pressures and problems, to extend the lifecycle as long as possible, and to find ways to renew your energy and interest in the work that comes your way. The difference between those who survive and those who succumb depends much upon the imagination and self-renewal that deans bring to their professional lives. Deans who live the longest find ways to sustain the joy of deaning.

The Ongoing Life of One Retired Dean

"How are you enjoying retirement, Tom?" This is the question I get everywhere I meet old friends and colleagues. "I read that nice article about your retirement in the local paper and see that the mayor even declared in a proclamation that this event was to be honored in the city as 'Dr. Thomas R. McDaniel Day,' and I see that the governor awarded you the Order of the Silver Crescent for your contributions to the state and region—very cool way to go out."

So, am I retired? Well, yes and no. Let me explain:

Yes, I am officially retired, as evidenced by the following:

1. The title *emeritus* follows my listing in the college catalogue in the roster of retired faculty.
2. I have been honored on my retirement by resolutions and awards from the faculty, the administration, the mayor, and the governor.
3. No longer do I get a monthly college paycheck and college benefits.
4. No more faculty or administrative meetings fill up my calendar.
5. I am drawing down on my TIAA retirement as well as Social Security to maintain our family's lifestyle.
6. After lunch, I take a long nap before *Judge Judy* comes on.

So, am I retired? Definitely, yes.

No, I am really not retired, as evidenced by the following:

1. I still go to work every day and have the same office, files, and computer I have had for years.
2. My course load of four courses for the year would, at most colleges, constitute a half-time position.

3. My schedule includes, just for the fall term, seven talks, guest lectures, civic club presentations, conference papers, and speeches.
4. I will continue to serve as executive editor of one professional journal and consulting editor of another.
5. A journal will be publishing an article I am writing titled "My Last Commencement Speech," and I have yet another article in mind.
6. I will continue with my teaching and mentoring duties at the college and for my church.

So, am I retired? Definitely, no.

As I have told those who ask what I am doing with my free time in retirement: "I don't hunt or fish, can't sing or paint, do not like to travel, and gave up golf." I would, as the saying goes, prefer to wear out rather than to rust out—so I choose to keep active with the very things I enjoyed doing when I was employed. And as I've quoted elsewhere in this book, "Old deans never die; they just lose their faculties." I want to keep my faculties alive and well.

As I reflect on the question—to retire or not to retire—I have concluded that this is a classic case of different strokes for different folks. For college professors, who are not wearing themselves out roofing houses or using jackhammers, this is a more perplexing question than it might be for others. Mandatory retirement was outlawed by the 1994 Age Discrimination Act, although colleges, since 1998, have been able to offer various incentives, such as phased retirement, an option I chose three years ago (our limit is three years at half-time).

How do others react to the retirement decision? I may be oversimplifying a complex decision, but many of my friends and neighbors fall into four categories:
1. Those who hate their work—10 minutes to adjust
2. Those who tolerate their work—10 days to adjust
3. Those who like their work—10 weeks to adjust
4. Those who are their work—never (this might be me!)

Deal with it, my friends, and more power to you if you make or have made different choices in your retirement.

Reflections of a Retired Dean

To serve a college or university as a dean or provost is a special honor and responsibility. I had the pleasure to be in such offices—department chair, division head, dean, vice president for academic affairs, provost, interim president, and (finally!) senior vice president—for a total of 45 years in the same liberal arts college. But I decided to retire in 2015 to let others take the lead in our shared academic enterprise and to devote more time to other academic pursuits. My administrative colleagues have been kind and supportive, even allowing me to retain my fine office suite and providing clerical support for ongoing projects.

Like many other former deans, I have had difficulties letting go of duties and friendships, but I think I have arrived at a happy compromise that might be a useful guide to other academic leaders who are leaving their institutions and wish to continue contributing to the college and the profession. Below are a few ways I have found to stay connected while leaving the heavy lifting (including countless committee, council, and taskforce meetings) to those who have assumed my responsibilities of office.

Scholarly work

Being retired gives me more time to write for a variety of journals, including *Academic Leader* and several others in my areas of academic interest. I have published in more than 60 different journals over the years and enjoy sending off manuscripts to some to my favorite publishers when an idea strikes me as worth examining through an article. Most of us, I believe, continue to have research and writing interests (even passions) and still have scholarly contributions to make to our fields.

Editing

Many journals welcome academics who want to serve as consulting editors, and this is satisfying academic work for many of us who like to contribute to the profession—whatever our disciplines might be. I have been particularly fortunate to be able to continue as an executive editor of a journal, which gives me the opportunity to stay abreast of the scholarship in my field. New ideas abound, and I enjoy seeing what other scholars are working on and deciding which submitted manuscripts may be of interest to others in our reading audience.

Conferences

Academic leaders are often reluctant to leave campus as their ongoing duties hold them in place, but retired leaders have much more freedom to travel to conferences, either to present or just to enjoy the stimulation and fellowship such conferences provide. Passing on the wisdom one has gained from experience (including mistakes as well as victories) is a special reward for retired deans. We want our successors to succeed!

Mentoring

Related to conference participation is the potential opportunity to give guidance and advice to young faculty members and new administrators in one's former institution—if you are fortunate enough to be staying in the same vicinity. I am currently helping an assistant professor in my field with ideas for articles and opportunities for other academic endeavors. This can be a real pleasure for one who has the time to assist those who follow in one's footsteps up the academic ladder of tenure and promotions and perhaps even into administration someday.

Speaking

Another activity that keeps me occupied and involved in my community is speaking at various civic and educational clubs and organizations. Unless they have retired to some barren wilderness or foreign desert, a retired academic leader will have ample opportunities to address community groups on subjects of interest both to the retiree and to the organization. Why not make use of all that stored knowledge and wisdom? No need to let it atrophy and disappear into the ether!

Teaching

Most if not all academic leaders entered the palace of administration through the courtyard of teaching; our talents and interests in academic and pedagogical enterprises are what attracted us to the profession at some early point in our careers. So why not return to that first love to teach a course or two in your former institution or some other college near your home? You might polish up a favorite course in your repertoire or even develop a new one, depending on the college's needs. You might even become a student again by auditing that fascinating-sounding art history or French culture course a colleague is teaching. In retirement we need to keep our faculties alive and well!

In the final analysis, retirement is what we make it; the choices are ours. Of course, there are travel, golf, the arts, and other leisure activities one has well earned. But the good news is that now we old deans (and other academic leaders) have that one commodity that seemed to be in critically short supply during our years of active service: time. I plan to use my time in a balanced way, with family vacations and travel, to be sure, but also by holding on to some of the experiences that were so satisfying during my working years. Perhaps you will as well when you decide to leave the groves of academe for the retired life.

Additional Resources from Magna Publications

BULK PURCHASES

To purchase multiple print copies of this book, please visit:
www.MagnaGroupBooks.com

MEMBERSHIPS/SUBSCRIPTIONS

Faculty Focus
www.facultyfocus.com
A free e-newsletter on effective teaching strategies for the college classroom.

Academic Leader Membership
www.Academic-Leader.com
Academic Leader covers the trends, challenges, and best practices today's academic decision-makers. Members gain access to the latest thinking in academic leadership and learn how peers at other institutions are solving problems, managing change, and setting direction. New articles are published throughout the month.

The Teaching Professor Membership
www.TeachingProfessor.com
The Teaching Professor is an annual membership that reflects the changing needs of today's college faculty and the students they teach. This new fully online version of the newsletter that faculty have enjoyed for more than 30 years includes the best of the print version—great articles and practical, evidence-based insights—but also many new features including video, graphics, and links that make it an even more indispensable resource.

CONFERENCES

Leadership in Higher Education Conference
www.AcademicLeadershipConference.com
The Leadership in Higher Education Conference provides higher-education leaders with an opportunity to expand leadership skills with proactive strategies, engaging networking, time-saving tips, and best practices.

The Teaching Professor Annual Conference
www.TeachingProfessorConference.com
This event provides an opportunity to learn effective pedagogical techniques, hear from leading teaching experts, and interact with colleagues committed to teaching and learning excellence. Join more than 1,000 educators from around the country.
Attendees hear from a roster of prestigious experts and nationally recognized thought leaders. A broad mix of plenary addresses, concurrent sessions, and timely roundtable discussions leave no topic untouched.

BOOKS

The Academic Leader's Handbook: A Resource Collection for College Administrators
https://www.amazon.com/dp/B0764KMC5Z
The Academic Leader's Handbook: A Resource Collection for College Administrators details an array of proven management strategies and will help further your achievements as a leader in higher education. Discover new leadership tools and insights at departmental, administrative, and executive levels.

Active Learning: A Practical Guide for College Faculty
https://www.amazon.com/dp/B071ZN8R32
Learn how to apply active learning methods in both small and large classes as well as in an online teaching environment. Whether you are new to active learning methods or experienced with them, this comprehensive reference book can guide you every step of the way.

The College Teacher's Handbook: A Resource Collection for New Faculty
https://www.amazon.com/dp/0912150688
The College Teacher's Handbook: A Resource Collection for New Faculty provides the essential tools and information that any new teacher in higher education needs to confidently lead a college classroom.

Essential Teaching Principles: A Resource Collection for Adjunct Faculty
https://www.amazon.com/dp/0912150246
This book provides a wealth of both research-driven and classroom-tested best practices to help adjuncts develop the knowledge and skills required to run a successful classroom. Compact and reader-friendly, this book is conveniently organized to serve as a ready reference whenever a new teaching challenge arises—whether it's refreshing older course design, overcoming a student's objection to a grade, or fine-tuning assessments.

Essential Teaching Principles: A Resource Collection for Teachers
https://www.amazon.com/dp/0912150580
This book serves as a quick and ready reference as you encounter the challenges of teaching college-level material in the high school classroom. For an AP or IB teacher, there's no better resource.

Faculty Development: A Resource Collection for Academic Leaders
https://www.amazon.com/dp/0912150661
Discover proven tips and insights, from top academic experts, that will help you enhance faculty development programming and training on your campus.

Flipping the College Classroom: Practical Advice from Faculty
https://www.amazon.com/dp/B01N2GZ61O
This collection is a comprehensive guide to flipping no matter how much—or how little—experience you have with it. If you are just getting started, you will learn where and how to begin. If you have been at it for a while, you will find new ideas to try and solutions to common challenges. *Flipping the College Classroom: Practical Advice from Faculty* is an invaluable resource that covers all the necessary territory.

Grading Strategies for the Online College Classroom: A Collection of Articles for Faculty
https://www.amazon.com/dp/0912150564
Do your grading practices accurately reflect your online students' performance? Do your assessment and feedback methods inspire learning? Are you managing the time you spend on these things—or is the workload overwhelming? *Grading Strategies for the Online College Classroom: A Collection of Articles for Faculty* can help you master the techniques of effective online grading—while avoiding some of the more costly pitfalls.

Helping Students Learn: Resources, Tools, and Activities for College Educators
https://www.amazon.com/dp/0912150602
This workbook is a must-have guide for faculty. While the roles in the college classroom often are defined by teachers teaching and students learning, the reality is that not many students have a clear understanding of how to learn.

Managing Adjunct Faculty: A Resource Collection for Administrators
https://www.amazon.com/dp/B01N2OVK5W
Chances are your adjunct population has been built on an ad hoc basis to fill instructional needs. As a result, your institution might not have a solid management framework to support them. That's a gap you can close with guidance from *Managing Adjunct Faculty: A Resource Collection for Administrators*. This invaluable guide offers an extensive review of best practices for managing an adjunct cohort and integrating them more fully into your campus community.

Teaching Strategies for the Online College Classroom: A Collection of Faculty Articles
https://www.amazon.com/dp/0912150483
Includes online teaching strategies ranging from building a successful start of the semester, fostering productive connections, managing challenging behavior in the online classroom, and enhancing student engagement.

Made in the USA
Monee, IL
03 May 2021

67533728R00075